YBOR CITY

Its Story in Pictures

★ ★ ★

YBOR CITY CIGAR CO.

"The Flor de Ybor City (Ybor City Cigar Co.) logo and trademark is owned, and officially licensed by, Fuente Marketing Ltd." The Cigar label bears the name of the historic community and is gratefully used with permission.

Cover: The Immigrant Statue by Steven Dickey in Centennial Park, dedicated 1992.

Phil Sauerbrun

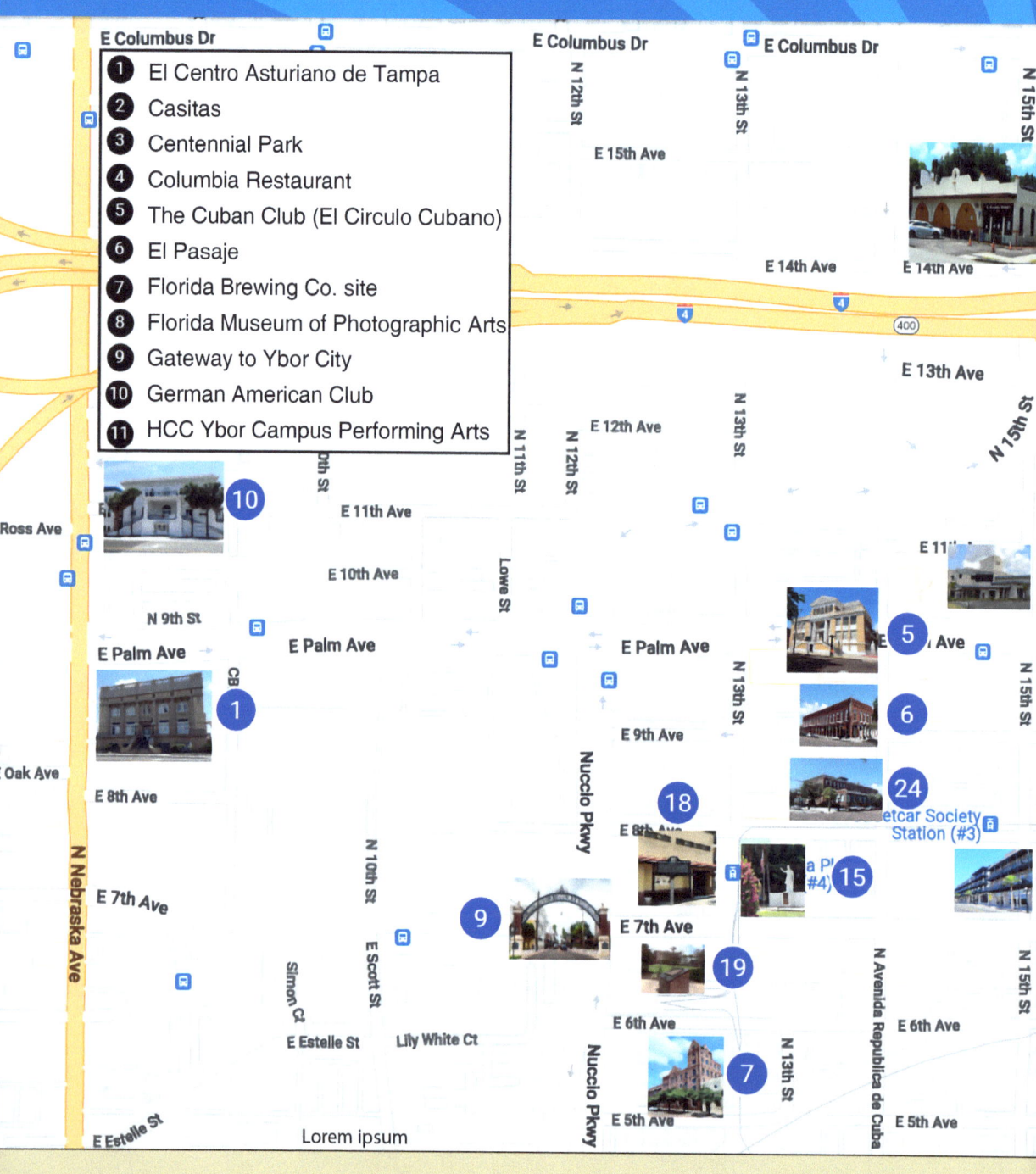

1. El Centro Asturiano de Tampa
2. Casitas
3. Centennial Park
4. Columbia Restaurant
5. The Cuban Club (El Circulo Cubano)
6. El Pasaje
7. Florida Brewing Co. site
8. Florida Museum of Photographic Arts
9. Gateway to Ybor City
10. German American Club
11. HCC Ybor Campus Performing Arts

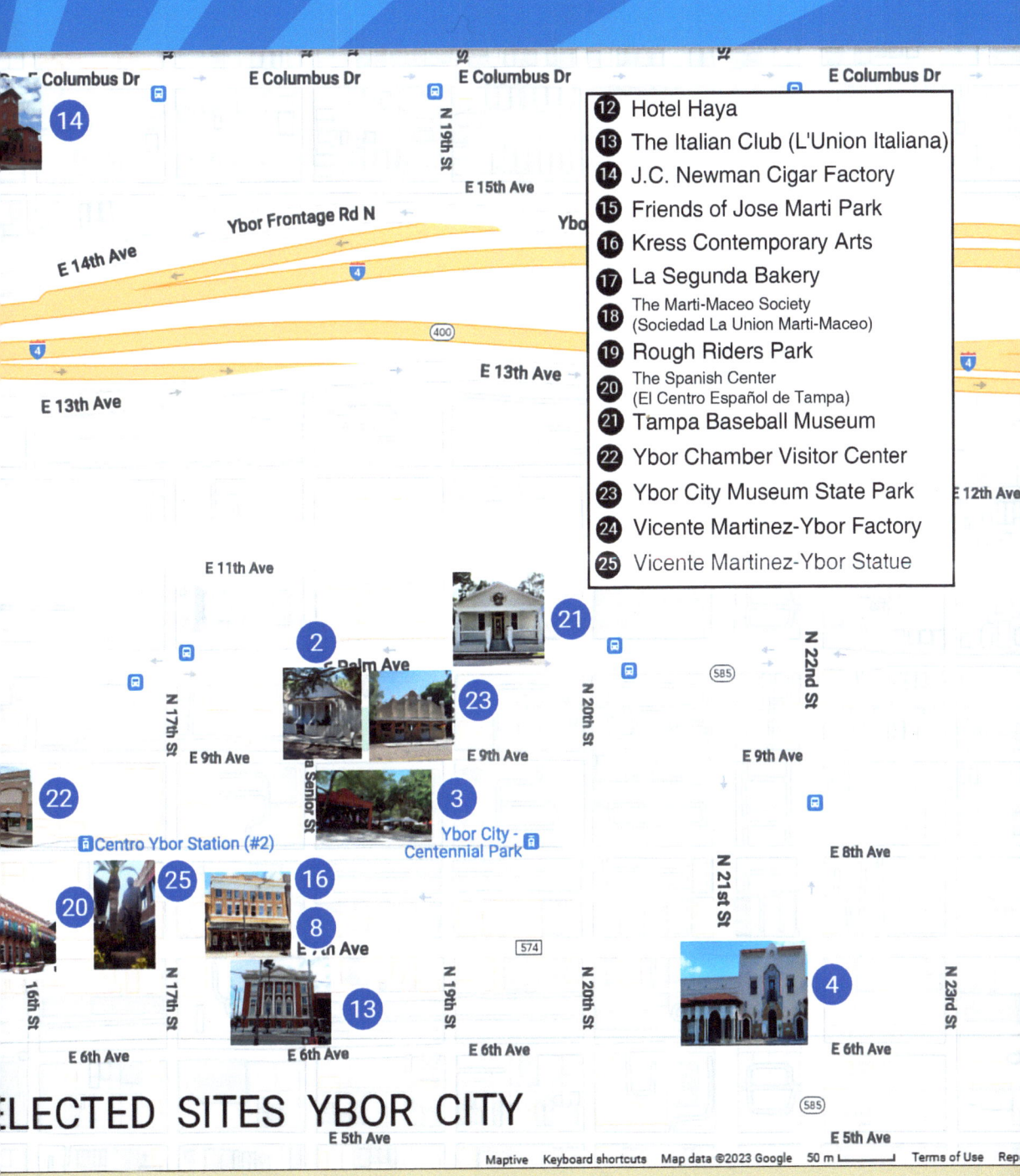

12	Hotel Haya
13	The Italian Club (L'Union Italiana)
14	J.C. Newman Cigar Factory
15	Friends of Jose Marti Park
16	Kress Contemporary Arts
17	La Segunda Bakery
18	The Marti-Maceo Society (Sociedad La Union Marti-Maceo)
19	Rough Riders Park
20	The Spanish Center (El Centro Español de Tampa)
21	Tampa Baseball Museum
22	Ybor Chamber Visitor Center
23	Ybor City Museum State Park
24	Vicente Martinez-Ybor Factory
25	Vicente Martinez-Ybor Statue

SELECTED SITES YBOR CITY

YBOR CITY
Its Story in Pictures

by Phil Sauerbrun

Editor: Laura Kaiser, Word Haven Editorial
Proofreaders: Cheryl Jaclin Isaac, CherylJI Editing, Rosalie Guarino Simms
Contributing editors: Tracy Midulla, Lucas Campoe
Cover Design and Formatting: Alejandro Ariel Martin, Bloom Design Agency
Marketing: Mary Walewski, Buy the Book Marketing

Grateful appreciation is extended to Joe King Carter, David Audet, and Ron Watson for the use of photographs of their art. The author is also indebted to the following photographers: PamElla Lee Photography, Dave Decker Photography, Keir Magoulas of Visit Tampa Bay, Arminda Mata, Scott M. Deitche, Michael A. Murphy, and the submission of images of the J.C. Newman Cigar Co. from Holden Rasmussen, the Italian Club from Mark Stanish, Jr., the galleries of Kress Contemporary from Tracy Midulla, the Tampa City Ballet from Paula Nuñez, the Cuban Sandwich Festival from Jolie Gonzalez-Padilla, the Tampa Bay Flamenco Dance Company from Maria Aurora Esparza, Ashley Smith of Wanderlusty Travel, Visit Tampa Bay Photo Library, Dysfunctional Grace from Liz Furlong, the Florida Museum of Photographic Arts through Lucas Campoe, and the images from the Hillsborough Community College Visual and Performing Arts Ybor Campus through Amanda J. Poss. These images and those of the author provided as a courtesy or under license copyright © 2024 may not be reproduced without their permission.

Maps by Maptive
Image above is the Ybor monogrammed medallion of 7th Avenue archway lights.
Comments may be directed to yborcityguide@gmail.com.

The author extends special thanks to Rosalie Simms, Joe King Carter, Tracy Midulla, Ron Watson, and Amanda J. Poss for their contributions and guidance, and to Jeff Sauerbrun for computer support. Special thanks to the following for picture description translations:
Italian – Sandra Alfieri, proofread by Angela Amenta
Spanish – Aimee Ponce, proofread by Sandra Alfieri

CONTENTS

Palm tree lined Seventh Avenue (La Setima), designated One of America's Ten Great Streets.

(by the American Planning Association, 2008). Seventh Avenue Street bricks restored in 2024.

INTRODUCTION

Centro Ybor District was established in 2000 to be a multipurpose business, dining, and entertainment center. Photo courtesy of Visit Tampa Bay, Keir Magoulas.

As the Ybor City Historic District of Tampa, Florida, approaches its 150th anniversary in 2036, this book seeks to capture its story in a series of photographs by subject. This book is not only for the visitor but also for those who know Ybor City well. It is a reference point to recall experiences and identify those opportunities for exploring Ybor City that you may have missed. If your interest is in museums and historical exhibits, you will find them grouped together. If you desire to experience Ybor City through tours that bring its past vividly to life, you will find many referenced here. Shops and marketplaces are identified, as well as various types of eating spots, including coffeehouses, craft beer establishments, pubs, restaurants, and eateries with live music. Whatever you enjoy most about Ybor City, this book will remind you of those moments and times. If you are a frequent visitor to Ybor City and have not seen some of these images, this book will inspire you to investigate further. Whether it be the ambience of an eatery or the pageantry and celebration of Ybor's many cultural events, this book will help shape your next visit.

This book is trilingual. Not only are all the pictures captioned in English, but they are also indexed in Spanish and Italian. I hope you enjoy this book, which has been so joyfully put together with the assistance of many people.

Visitors to Ybor City are welcomed at the Chamber of Commerce Visitor Information Center (the VIC) and Gift Shop located at 1600 E. 8th Avenue, Suite B-104, (813) 241-8838, where a fully qualified staff is available to answer all questions regarding Ybor City and Tampa—what to see, how to get there, where to eat based on your preferences, and what it will cost. Best wishes for great experiences in Ybor City.

THE FOUNDER'S VISION

Following the US possession of Florida from Spain in 1821, Fort Brooke was built at the mouth of the Hillsborough River in 1824, within what is today downtown Tampa. From 1824 until the 1880s, the population was as low as 800 as inhabitants fought to possess the area, which had belonged to the Indigenous people for thousands of years and was subject to yellow fever, heat, and marshy surroundings teeming with mosquitoes, snakes, and alligators. It was a settlement looking for deliverance.

Left, **Vicente Martinez-Ybor**, circa 1890. Tampa History Center, P.D.-US.

Right, **statue of Ybor** in Centro Ybor, courtesy of Dave Decker Photography.

In 1885 a man named Vicente Martinez-Ybor (1818-1896) came to look at the area for cigar production. He had operated his cigar business in well-organized labor locations in Key West and New York. In the mid-1880s an extended strike took place in Key West, which was his primary manufacturing location at the time, and many cigar rollers working in the factories there moved to other locations. Cigar production in Key West was severely crippled. [1] General strikes by well-organized labor frequently closed down all factory operations—even those like Ybor's, which may not have been responsible for the conditions that caused the strike. Strikes frequently impacted his years of business in the cigar industry.

Two business acquaintances of Ybor's from New York looked at the Tampa area in 1885 for investment opportunities in the growing of guava, and they stopped by Key West on the way back to New York to tell Ybor about the opportunities for cigar production in Tampa. One was Gavino Gutierrez, a businessperson and engineer by training. Soon Ybor and Ignacio Haya, a fellow cigar producer, made the trip by steamer to Tampa. They saw the possibilities in an emerging little hamlet as the railroad was being extended southward to Tampa, by Henry B. Plant, which would give access to the area by both shipping and rail. [3]

Vicente Martinez-Ybor's vision for his cigar manufacturing business was to develop a new location for production without the initial presence of organized labor, where he would have the opportunity to create trust with his employees. He reasoned that he would not only be able to meet their needs of employment but would be able to create a community environment where workers would be content and flourish. [4] Even though Tampa suffered the effects of yellow fever and marshy mosquito-filled real estate complete with snakes and alligators, his vision would give Tampa its reason for being after a more than sixty-year struggle to survive.

After his purchase of land, Ybor had his new acreage surveyed by Gutierrez and began clearing the land and constructing his first wooden factory building with the assistance of Gutierrez and Haya and with his factory administrator and partner, Eduardo Manrara, in late 1885. A construction boom ensued in the first ten years, as Ybor sought to create the manufacturing environment he envisioned. By the time of his death, in 1896, just over ten years later, he had built hundreds of homes for cigar workers, called *casitas*, pictured *next page*, a practice followed by other factory owners. He sold them just above his cost with no interest loans, allowing many cigar workers to own homes for the first time. He invited many of his competitors to come to Tampa and assisted some of them in the construction of their factories. His primary motivation was creating a work environment where all participants were benefited and satisfied. [5] By the time of his death, he had developed an infrastructure that included a streetcar system, enhanced the port of Tampa, improved the water supply, established beer production, initiated brick-laid roads, established sewer and water systems, and brought doctors to address the health needs of a cigar workforce that was increasing by the week. [6] In December 1896, when Don Vicente died in Ybor City, his vision had been largely accomplished. The population was approaching 15,000 and commerce was booming.

Courtesy of Keir Magoulas, Visit Tampa Bay

Completed in 1886, **Ybor's factory**, *above*, was the largest cigar factory in the world at that time. The cupola still remains astride the roof of the building in which an employee would be perched to watch for tobacco ships arriving from Cuba. The sighting of such a ship would initiate a race by the employee to Port Tampa in time to obtain the tobacco his employer's factory needed for cigar production.

This book presents a pictorial story of how goals became a reality not only for Ybor but also for Tampa and Florida. It is a story that reveals the life created by numerous cultures being brought together and ignited by the possibilities of living in a free society that would be of their own making.

RECALLING THE PAST

Museums and Exhibits

Ybor City is fortunate to have several centers of information from which tourists can learn about the history of how the cigar industry jump-started the development of the Tampa Bay area and the unique social and cultural character that was created and lives on today.

The Ybor City Museum State Park, *below,* located on 9ᵗʰ Avenue across from Centennial Park, is housed in the historic Ferlita Bakery, which operated at this site from the turn of the 20ᵗʰ century until the 1960s. The museum includes artifacts of Ybor City's early history, as well as photo, video, audio, and written presentations about the founding and development of Ybor City and the cigar industry. It illuminates the multicultural heritage of Ybor City. [7]

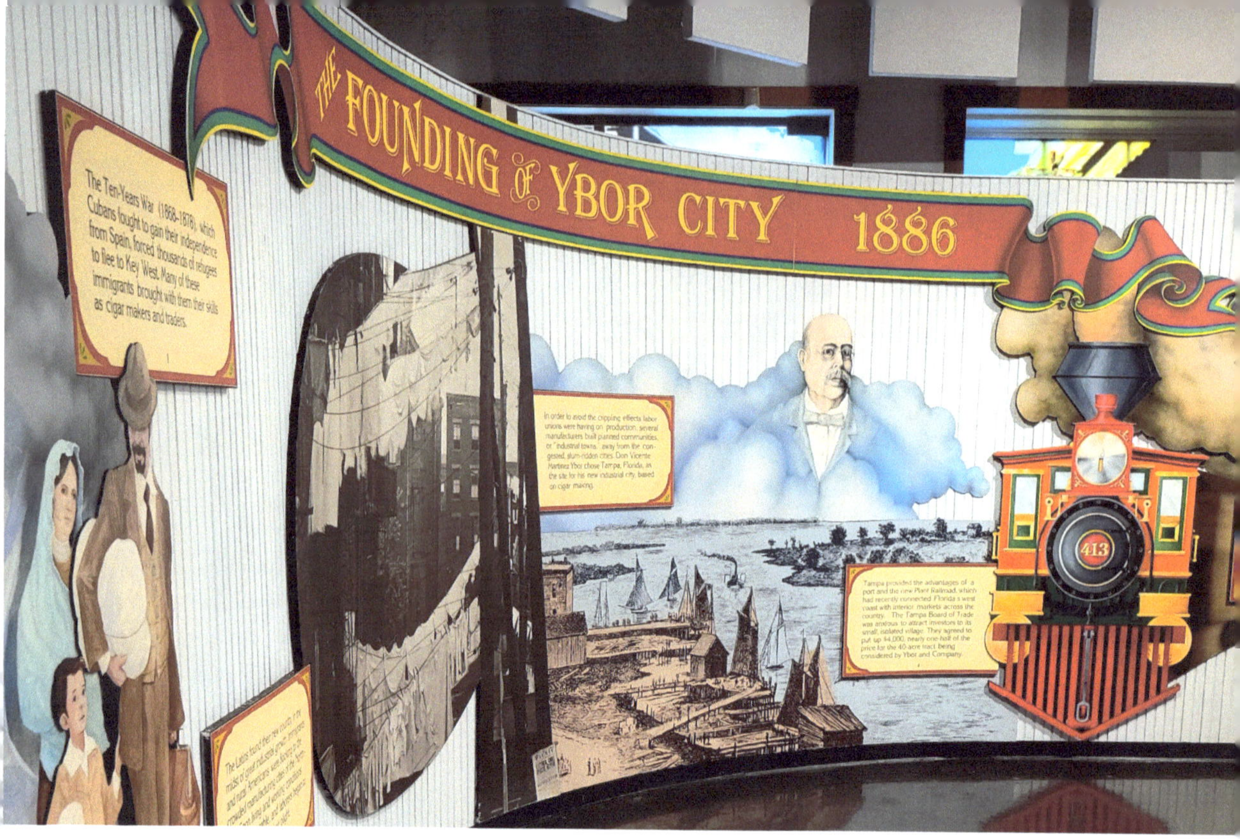

Museum exhibits document the story of Ybor City.

A vintage cigar rolling desk against the backdrop photo of a crowded cigar rolling factory floor inside an Ybor City factory c. 1920. Factory image, from the Historical Collection Tampa-Hillsborough County Public Library, P.D.-US.

Right, the **Ybor Seal** created by historian Anthony (Tony) P. Pizzo representing the nationalities of those who emigrated to Ybor City. Courtesy of Arminda Mata, President and CEO, Ybor City Museum Society.

The **Museum Garden**, *below*, adjacent to the museum, is an ornamental garden, which includes plants native to Florida. A bust of Vicente Martinez-Ybor is in the garden. Picnic tables and seating make it a popular setting for lunch. The garden can also be rented for special occasions.

Left, the **bust of Vicente Martinez-Ybor** in the Museum Garden.

Adjacent to the Museum Garden is a row of casitas, one of which is part of the **Casita Tour,** furnished as one would have been at the turn of the twentieth century.

Below, living quarters of a casita, courtesy of Ashley Smith, My Wanderlusty Life travel blog.

The J.C. Newman Cigar Co., *below*, located at 2701 N 16th Street and E Columbus Drive, is known historically as El Reloj, The Clock, which kept the Ybor City community on time with its iconic clock tower. It is the last remaining cigar factory not only in Ybor City but also in the country at large. The factory's current operation is a step back in time revealing what Ybor City was like when there were more than 200 large cigar factories during its heyday. The original building was completed in 1910, making the facility a museum in itself. The company has been in business since 1895. Its move to Ybor City in the mid 1950s marks an important step in a resurgence that would recognize the historical significance of the community and lead to national historic district designation in 1990. [8]

Above left, foyer of the J.C. Newman Cigar Co. factory and *right,* its museum. Below, the J.C. Newman Cigar Co. keeps the factory hand rolling legacy of cigar production alive. Courtesy of J.C. Newman Cigar Co.

Above, the **Tampa Baseball Museum**, N. 19th Street. Courtesy of Chantal Hevia

The Tampa Baseball Museum at the Al Lopez House, adjacent to the Ybor City Museum State Park, features the 135-year history of baseball in the Tampa area. It portrays the more than eighty professional players from the Bay area, among them some of the most famous in baseball history. The museum is housed in the home of Al Lopez, Tampa's first Major League player, manager, and National Baseball Hall of Fame inductee, which was moved to the Historic District during interstate highway construction.

Baseball came to be an integral part of the fabric of the immigrant community as the various cultural organizations established teams to compete with one another beginning in the 1880s. [9]

Left, main museum floor; *right*, Lou Piniella display. Courtesy of Arminda Mata, President & CEO of the Ybor City Museum Society.

The **Ybor City Chamber of Commerce Visitor Information Center (the VIC),** located on 8th Avenue in Centro Ybor, has historical exhibits, a video introducing the Historic District to visitors, and a gift shop. In addition, the VIC provides helpful information about the Historic District and Tampa. Trained tourism counselors guide visitors through a litany of options, including accommodations, streetcar travel, guided tours, museums, dining, and the arts scene of Ybor City and Tampa. [10]

The Visitor Information Center, (the VIC) is located at the rear east end of the Spanish Community Center on 8th Avenue with the streetcar line visible in front.

The theatre area at the VIC, which plays the orientation video.

Map of historic sites at the Visitor Information Center.

Left is a **carved wooden statue of Queen Isabella** that was commissioned by Vicente Martinez-Ybor to promote the Spanish influence and nature of the cigar industry. She was transported throughout the US and beyond for fairs and expositions. She stands on a round globe of the world, which is placed on top of a humidor that was used to store cigars.

The statue resides in Centro Asturiano de Tampa, inside the front entance of the building at 1913 N. Nebraska Ave.

Image courtesy of Crystal Blackwell-Lastra.

THE CULTURAL CLUBS

The story of Ybor City tells how multiple cultural and ethnic groups came together to make up the cigar economy. A number of these groups established community centers known as mutual-aid societies to form a supportive environment for immigrants. The main groups included Spanish, Hispanic Cubans, Afro Cubans, Italians, Sicilians, Romanians, Germans, and Eastern European Jews. There are six community centers that are identified in this section, four of which are active. All are within a mile radius. For a small monthly membership fee, these community centers provided medical care, recreation and fitness facilities, education classrooms in a variety of subjects including the English language, and canteens for light meals and refreshments. The medical clinics that they housed were the precursor to modern-day HMOs. A lifetime insurance policy existed from the cradle to the grave in many of the mutual-aid societies for the dues-paying members. Additionally, lavish ballrooms were included on the premises for social events and cultural celebrations.

The first community center was **Centro Español de Tampa**, established in 1891 using a building that was Vicente Martinez-Ybor's first wooden structure cigar factory. The community was composed of men originally from Spain. It was the predecessor for the community centers that followed. Today it serves as the location for restaurants. The current structure dates from 1912 and has Moorish architectural elements. It is the second building on the site. [11]

Centro Español de Tampa at 7th Avenue and 16th Street in Centro Ybor. Courtesy of Tampa AGS Media. See Picture Index for license

Historic marker, located on 8th Avenue at the rear of El Centro Español.

Above, the historic marker documents the creation of the mututal-assistance centers in the late 19th and early 20th centuries.

El Circulo Cubano, the Cuban Club, at Palm Avenue on 14th Street, was created from a union of a number of Cuban immigrant groups in 1902. The current building, shown *below*, dating from 1917-1918, replaced the previous structure that burned. The building contained a theatre, pharmacy, library, ballroom, and cantina among other amenities, which provided a meeting place to bring the Cuban community together. Conversations among members often centered around what was going on back in the home country, Cuba. This club currently has an active membership with special events in its stately interiors. [12]

 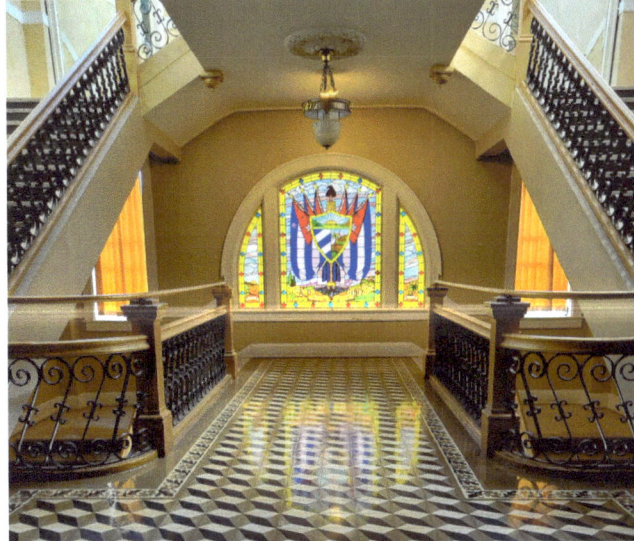

Left, **the Cuban Club** on 14th Street at Palm Avenue with a bust of José Martí on the right. *Right,* the Cuban coat of arms on the stained glass window near the ballroom of the Cuban Club.

El Centro Asturiano de Tampa, *on the next two pages*, located at E. Palm Avenue and N. Nebraska Avenue, was formed in 1902. Many Spanish immigrants came from Asturias, a province in Northern Spain on the Bay of Biscay. Today, its active membership includes descendants of Asturian immigrants, as many family lines trace back to Spain. This community center was an extension of El Centro Asturiano de La Habana, which was instrumental in establishing health benefits for the American branch.

Below, a group tour from Buildings Alive led by Cristal Lastra, President of the Centro Asturiano Board of Directors; Centro Asturiano's refurbished theatre, and its exterior at night. Courtesy of Arminda Mata, President and CEO, Ybor City Museum Society.

El Centro Asturiano de Tampa provided a hospital, medical insurance, and a cemetery for its members, exemplifying its cradle-to-the-grave support for its members. Today, its ballroom is used for special events, including wedding receptions and other celebrations. The building dates back to 1914. [13]

Sociedad la Union Martí-Maceo was created due to the Jim Crow laws that separated Hispanic Cubans from Afro Cubans based on race. It is named after two heroes of the Cuban Independence Movement. In Cuba, their communities were not segregated. While racial discrimination existed in Cuba, the Hispanic and Afro Cubans were not separated socially when they arrived in the United States which could have served as a model of race relations for the country at that time. However, state Jim Crow laws and the Supreme Court case of Plessy v. Ferguson reinforced separation of the races resulting in the removal of Black Cubans from the Cuban Club in 1899. Two groups of Afro Cubans were founded in 1900 and 1904 subsequently merging into the present organization. They were also separated from American Black people by language and religion, which made their social organization a vital support system for their community. [14]

Left, **the Society of Martí-Maceo**, E. 7th Avenue off the Nuccio Parkway. *Below,* **painted tile mural** on front of building by Carol Baker Curtiss of San Do Designs, Tampa.

The present location of the Society on E. 7th Avenue at the Gateway to Ybor City dates back to 1968 when its previous facility was the victim of urban renewal. The Afro Cuban community was extremely supportive of the Cuban Revolutionary movement in the nineteenth century for an independent Cuba and played a vital role in the armed forces for the Cuban Revolution of 1895-1898. The war became known in the United States as the Spanish-American War when the US entered the war in 1898.

The Italian Club on the corner of E. 7th Avenue at 18th Street, courtesy of Scott M. Deitche.

L'Unione Italiana, the Italian Club, *above*, was the second mutual-assistance center and was organized in 1894 by a charter group of Italians primarily from Sicily. It has occupied its beautiful premises on E. 7th Avenue at 18th Street since 1918 following a fire which destroyed its previous facility across the street. The building includes elements of the Greek Revival style with Italian and French Renaissance features. The cartouche above the second-floor windows depicts an oculus, a round eye-like disc, which anticipates the future and is supported by cornucopias representing the abundant life of America.

The Italian Club featured numerous amenities for its members and is very active today. Medical care took place in a neighboring clinic building. Within the walls of the club were classrooms, a library, recreational equipment, a theatre, cantina, and a beautiful ballroom. In 1934, the West Tampa Sicilian Club merged with the Ybor City Italian Club giving the club its current name and increased membership. The Italian Club, like its sister community centers, has imposing facilities which can be rented for special events. [15]

Below left, Second floor Lobby of the Italian Center at Christmas. *Below right*, the Connie Spoto Walter Theater, a gathering crowd, the prelude to a wedding. Below, the Capitano Grand Ballroom, a rehearsal for an event. Courtesy of the Italian Club, Mark Stanish.

Deutsch Amerikanischer Verein, the German-American Club, organized in 1901, was the mutual-assistance center not only for Germans, but for Eastern Europeans, including Romanians and Jews. Its current building, located on N. Nebraska Avenue at E. 11th Avenue, was known in the pre-World War years for having a popular restaurant featuring German cuisine. The First World War led to the decline and closing of this center in 1919 and its space is now utilized for special occasions. An addition has been built, which augments the facility's use as an inclusive health center, mirroring the medical clinic purposes of early twentieth century mutual-assistance centers. [16]

Front of **German American Club** with medical clinic to the left.

South side of building on 11th Avenue **showing architectural features**.

CASITAS
(little houses)

★ ★ ★

Casitas, located on 9th Avenue. The Ybor City Chamber of Commerce occupies the house on the corner.

The construction of casitas by Vicente Martinez-Ybor was an integral part of his strategy to create a healthy, satisfying environment for the cigar workers who were essential to the labor-intensive cigar industry. The housing he developed had many features making them comfortable living spaces for the incoming cigar workers who began to arrive in 1886. The houses were "shotgun" in design with a hallway running from the front door to the rear of the building for improved airflow. Roofs were designed to retain water, which was stored within the premises and prevented mosquito access. The multistep stairwell in front prevented entry by alligators and snakes. Screens and netting over the beds provided protection from mosquitoes. Of the thousands of casitas built in Ybor City, many still exist today as residences as well as businesses. Ybor City historian Wallace Reyes, PhD, writes that Ybor and his colleagues built more than 15,000 housing units, which included not only casitas, but bungalows and two-story houses. [17]

STREETCAR AND RAIL

Crew and train of Tampa Street Railway, 1886, State Archives of Florida, Florida Memory Collection, P.D. See Picture Index for license.

According to Ybor historian Wallace Reyes, the growing success of the cigar industry propelled economic development on many fronts. Henry B. Plant pushed the rail line southward from Jacksonville to Sanford and from there to Tampa, reaching the sleepy little township in August 1885. To spur rail development, Ybor and his partner, Manrara, purchased controlling interest in a rail company; rail service between Ybor City and Tampa was established in April 1886. Soon streetcars operated on a regular schedule between the two communities. [18]

Henry B. Plant extended his rail line down to Port Tampa, the initial port for Tampa. He built two hotels at Port Tampa to handle the influx of immigrants in the 1880s and the first decade of the twentieth century. Port Tampa became the Ellis Island processing center for the area, with a rail line that ran from Port Tampa all the way to New York. The streetcars then and now were constructed on train car chassis, a process which has changed little since it was first instituted. The first streetcars operated on a narrow-gauge track with small woodburning steam engines pulling the cars, as shown on the *previous page*. [19]

TECO Line cars in the Ybor City maintenance yard, from Railfann99. See Picture Index for license.

Advancements in rail transportation spurred the growth of the cigar industry, which led to further improvements in local and regional rail transportation. *Above* is the rail yard maintenance facility for the Heritage Streetcar System, located in Ybor City. The streetcar system was reinstated in 2002 after being discontinued after World War II and has, once again, become an essential link between Tampa and its Fourth Ward, Ybor City. [20] The current streetcars will be replaced by redesigned rail cars in the near future, which will provide better accessibility and move at higher speeds. The streetcar line operates out of eleven stations, four of which are in Ybor City with the remaining seven located in Tampa proper. It is one of the few urban transit systems that provides ridership at no cost. *Below* is the vintage wood interior of the heritage streetcar.

Interior of a TECO car, 2020, Peter K. Burian. See Picture Index for license.

The street car route operates between downtown Tampa and Ybor City on a single track with passing sidings at frequent intervals as shown on the *next page*. Courtesy of Keir Magoulas, Visit Tampa Bay.

The reestablishment of Tampa's architecturally striking Union Station, shown on the *next page*, on the outskirts of Ybor City, has been marked by increasing Amtrak ridership. The station is poised for further transportation improvements in the future. With the Brightline initiative for rapid transit and new transportation hubs gaining momentum, the connection of Miami, Orlando, and Tampa by high-speed rail service ensures that rail transportation will continue to be a part of Tampa's history and development.

Restored to its former glory in 1998, the 1912 Tampa **Union Station** is a landmark structure reflecting the Italian Renaissance Revival style. Courtesy of Tampa AGS Media. See Picture Index for license.

THE COLUMBIA RESTAURANT

Arguably the most significant landmark in Ybor City, the Columbia Restaurant could earn that designation for many reasons. Today, it is the largest Spanish restaurant in the United States with fifteen dining rooms and a seating capacity of 1,700. Its history dates to 1905, with a salad on its menu with the name "1905," in honor of the year. Occupying an entire block in Ybor City on 7th Avenue and 21st Street, the restaurant interiors take one back to the bygone era of the early twentieth century when Ybor City was referred to as "the Cigar Capital of the World." With its timeless furnishings, including paintings, sculptures, tiled floors, and mosaic walls, as well as its chandeliers, stained glass, and other antiques, the establishment is a timeless representation of the heyday of Ybor City.

Five generations of the Hernandez-Gonzmart family have carefully made their marks on the establishment without infringing on the contributions of previous generations. The dining rooms, added over the more than one hundred-year history of the restaurant, have their own themes. **The Don Quixote Dining Room** recalls the classic novel by Miguel de Cervantes. The main character, Don Quixote de la Mancha, tilts at windmills in his quest to restore the chivalric age of Spain. The tile murals, inside as well as the exterior, tell the story of an insensible quest to restore the dignity and honor of Spain's chivalric past. *Below* is an **outdoor tile mural** picturing the man of la Mancha. [21]

The artwork presents a symbolic parallel with the story of the restaurant's commitment to Ybor City by its continual expansion in facilities during years when the Ybor City district was in sharp decline. The images from the novel similarly reflect the restaurant's embracing the uncertain future by recalling the past glory days of Ybor City. The restaurant's dedication to the future made it a forerunner heralding a time of restoration as early as the late 1930s, decades before revitalization began.

Below is the impressive **El Patio Dining Room**, a breathtaking place to dine. From its skylight to its mezzanine balconies to its patio floor, each seating location is an uplifting experience. There is a large sculpture reproduced from a sculpture discovered in the ruins of Pompeii. The lighting, airiness and décor of this room creates an ambience of peace and tranquility. [22] The glories of the past and hopefulness for the future become merged in this timeless space. The dining room was added in 1937 by Casimiro Hernandez, Jr. when the cigar industry was in full decline.

Above, **El Patio Room**, courtesy of the Columbia Restaurant.

Above, the outdoor tile façade of the **Columbia Restaurant** on 7ᵗʰ Avenue.

Columbia Restaurant's lighted corner on 7th Avenue at 21st Street beckons diners as evening approaches.

A HOTBED OF REVOLUTION

The Cuban Revolution of 1895 was the third attempt in the nineteenth century to break Cuba free from Spanish control. In that year, Cuba and Puerto Rico were the last remnants of Spanish colonial rule in the New World. The Spanish presence in Cuba had become quite oppressive in order to crack down on the independence movement on the island. The effort to free Cuba was led by José Martí, the voice of the independence movement. By the time of the 1895 revolution, he had established himself in the Western Hemisphere as a poet, lawyer, playwright, and charismatic, impassioned speaker on behalf of freeing Cuba, as well as a contributor to political thought. His diplomatic efforts throughout the Americas earned him the reference as a "statesman of Latin America."

Right, is his statue in the Friends of José Martí Park in Ybor City, courtesy of Dave Decker Photography and *left* Photo of José Martí taken by 1895, unknown source and author, P.D.-U.S. .

Martí's planning encompassed raising funds for the revolutionary movement throughout the Americas. His strongest financial support came from the cigar workers of Ybor City. Martí is recorded as making approximately twenty trips to Ybor City in the first half of the 1890s. Shown *below* is Martí speaking to the Cuban cigar workers on the steps of Vicente Martinez-Ybor's cigar factory. Ybor was a well-known supporter of a "free" Cuba. Alleged Spanish agents attempted to assassinate José Martí by poisoning in Ybor City in December 1892. Martí survived to continue his critical work in which he is pictured *below* passionately imploring the cigar workers to become involved in the impending revolution. In 1895 Martí was determined to be inserted into the military effort even though he had no military training. After years of planning by Martí, two insurgent groups landed in Eastern Cuba, one led by Afro Cuban General Antonio Maceo and a second led by General Máximo Gómez and José Martí. He disembarked from the Dominican Republic with General Gómez and arrived on the southeast coast of Cuba in April 1895. [23]

In this 1893 photo, **Martí** is in the center with an open coat and white shirt, with cigar workers from the Ybor factory. José Martí on the iron steps of Vicente Martinez-Ybor's factory, circa 1890, State Archives of Florida, Florida Memory Collections. See Picture Index for license.

The Cuban Revolution was underway in the month following their landings when José Martí was killed in a skirmish with Spanish troops at Dos Rios River in May. While the immediate reaction to his death was traumatic for the insurgency, it served to galvanize the revolutionary forces such that by 1898, they were approaching the outskirts of Havana. The United States sent the *USS Maine* to Havana Harbor to protect American interests and collect any American citizens seeking to leave. However, in February, the ship blew up in the harbor. This event precipitated the entry of the United States into the war, which became known as the Spanish-American War. [24]

Tampa and Ybor City became the staging point for the American war effort as more than 30,000 troops descended on Ybor City and Tampa, many camping near where the Columbia Restaurant exists today. The logistics of trying to accommodate such an influx placed Tampa squarely on the map as a strategic Florida municipality on the rise. In June 1898, Theodore Roosevelt, head of American forces known as the "Rough Riders," paraded with his troops down 7th Avenue in Ybor City before heading to waiting ships at Port Tampa. With the arrival of US troops in Cuba in the summer of 1898, the war was over in three months as Spanish resistance collapsed. Cuba had won its independence. Now it had to establish the democratic government envisioned by José Martí. [25] On the *next page,* **Lt. Colonel Theodore Roosevelt** stands on San Juan Hill, Cuba, after its capture by his "Rough Riders" during the Spanish-American War.

Enter into the park and you are on Cuban soil. The Friends of José Martí Park, courtesy of Keir Magoulas, Visit Tampa Bay.

Lt. Colonel Roosevelt and his Rough Riders at the top of San Juan Hill in Santiago de Cuba, July 1898. William Dinwiddie, Library of Congress Prints and Photographs Division. P.D.-US.

Above,, **Memorial Plaque**, Rough Riders Park, Ybor City.

A SKILLED CRAFT

★ ★ ★

Cigar shops abound on and just off 7th Avenue in Ybor City, like Tabanero, pictured *below*. Many have rollers in the front window so passersby can watch the process of cigar creation from beginning to end. Add a tip to the tip jar and you'll hear more about the age-old process of the skilled craft of cigar making by hand and you'll be told that handmade cigars are of the highest quality.

Below is a woman rolling cigars at **La Faraona cigar shop**, where she sits at her rolling desk making a cigar from the beginning of the process to the final product. Yes, women rolled cigars over one hundred years ago and still do today, as the owner will attest.

The cigar shops of Ybor City offer many opportunities to learn about this important element in Latin culture. Some offer a barista who serves café con leche, beer, or wine to visitors who are welcomed to have a moment to relax and escape the summer heat. The visitor can arrange to see a shop's humidor, a humidity-controlled environment ranging from a cabinet to a large vault-like room where cigars are stored until purchase. Many of the shops offer souvenirs for tourists as a memento of their visit.

At J.C. Newman Cigar Co., the last remaining factory that resembles manufacturing on a mass production level, is an opportunity to see how cigars are made by machine, *above*, as well as by hand, *top*. During the heyday of cigar production in Ybor City, before the Great Depression, cigars were made exclusively by hand. Tours lead attendees through the factory and its museum to witness the creative skill of making cigars both by hand and machine. The cigar shops in Ybor City reflect an age-old practice that evolved into the modern-day craft where smoking tobacco leaves tightly wrapped together dates back to the Indigenous people of the land Europeans came to call America. Cigar making became a critical component of the Latin culture and was transported back to Spain, England, and Holland by their explorers.

This critical element of cigar production in the Latin American culture of Ybor City can be experienced at numerous cigar shop locations in addition to the factory at J.C. Newman. These shops include La Faraona Cigars, La Herencia de Cuba Cigars, Long Ash Cigars, Nicahabana Cigars, Tabanero Cigars, Tampa Sweethearts Cigar Co., Tampero Cigars, and Ybor Cigars Plus.

Below, a **modern-day humidor** with individual lockers for customers at Tabanero Cigars.

Bottom left, Arturo Fuente offices in its original factory building. *Bottom right*, the corporate logo on the adjacent warehouse. Both buildings have undergone renovation and restoration.

GUIDED TOURS

★ ★ ★

Ybor City is a more recent addition to America's historic districts. Its story relies, in part, on excellent tours to educate, in an entertaining way, about the significance and contribution of Ybor City. Tours are conducted by dynamic and knowledgeable leaders who are experts on their subjects. Those interested in a tour of Ybor City can either go online to reserve a tour date and time or call in advance.

Below, Holden Rasmussen, historian for the J.C. Newman Cigar Co., conducts his **tour through the factory** showing the process of making a cigar beginning in the museum of J.C. Newman Factory.

A **cigar factory tour** is conducted at **J.C. Newman Cigar Co.** factory, the last remaining factory to manufacture cigars in the United States. Its operation in many ways resembles the mass production by human assembly line of early twentieth century cigar factories. The tour includes observing cigars made by hand rolling and by machine which came more into use in the 1930s. The factory's operation is reminiscent of the volume in which cigars were made in Ybor City in the early twentieth century when more than 200 large cigar factories produced cigars by hand rolling. The daily tours are replete with stories recounting the early years of Ybor City in what was originally the Regensburg factory. [29]

Max Herman, of Tampa Bay Tours, begins the Ybor City Historic Walking Tour at the statue of Vicente Martinez-Ybor in Centro Ybor on 7th Avenue near 16th Street. Tours are conducted most days of the week. In the evenings, the company also conducts the Ybor City Ghost Tour replete with history of people who have passed on to the other side—but perhaps not entirely—as you visit buildings that are on America's most haunted list. The Downtown Tampa Historical Walking Tour identifies all the elements of Tampa's remarkable development that make it a truly unique urban area. [26]

Max Herman gestures to El Pasaje, originally Vicente Martinez-Ybor's office building, during an evening ghost tour. Courtesy of Tampa Bay Tours.

Cindi Hughlett speaks to a **Food Tour** group at the VIC.

The Ybor City Food Tour is another way to experience Ybor City. Not only does it focus on the food and its evolution in Ybor City, but it also places the tastes and smells of dining there within its historical context. The many different cultural and ethnic groups that came to Ybor City are as much distinguished by their food as other cultural characteristics. This tour operates most days of the week, and its fee includes the cost of dining at a number of eateries in the Ybor City Historic District. [27] Don Vicente Martinez-Ybor's bronze statue in Centro Ybor is the starting point for a number of tours in Ybor City.

The Tampa Mafia Tour is conducted several times each month with the exception of the summer months. It meets at King Corona Cigars and Café on 7th Avenue and is not to be missed for its chilling tales of a huge cast of criminal ne'er-do-wells and the impact they had on Tampa and Ybor City. The Kefauver and McClellan Congressional Committees helped to expose Mafia operations in Tampa. One whole volume of the Kefauver Report is of testimony taken in Tampa, Florida, in the 1950s. The tours are often conducted by **Scott M. Deitche**, the noted authority and expert on the Mafia in the United States, including Tampa and Ybor City. Pictured *below*, his tour begins on 7th Avenue at King Corona Cigars and Café. [28]

CRAFT BREWING

★ ★ ★

Ybor City is a community of many firsts in Florida, including beer production. Vicente Martinez-Ybor's biographer, Loy Glenn Westfall, writes that the transport of water to housing was problematic because there were few potable water sources and people would have to carry it a long way home. Ybor was instrumental in getting beer production started in Ybor City to compensate for the inconvenience of accessing water. He placed his partner and administrator, Eduardo Manrara, in charge of establishing beer manufacturing in Ybor City. Manrara met with German immigrants to develop the Florida Brewing Company, founded by Ybor and Manrara. The building, *next page*, was the brewery constructed in 1896 to manufacture beer and was the first brewery in Florida. At six stories, it was the tallest building in Florida for many years and it continues to be the tallest building in Ybor City. It encompasses many layers of brick on its exterior and interior walls to make the building as cool as possible for the beer processes. It was completed in 1896, the year Vicente Martinez-Ybor died. The brewery produced beer until the early 1960s when operations ceased due to competition from larger beer companies and the loss of its major export market, Cuba, when the embargo was instituted. [30]

The building fell into disrepair and was abandoned until attorney Dale Swope with co-owner/contractor Joseph Kokolakis renovated the building at great expense and utilized it for his law firm in 1999. The building has another connection with Florida history. Theodore Roosevelt and the Rough Riders celebrated the victory of the Spanish-American War by having a beer at the brewery's location at 1234 E. 5th Avenue. The building was erected at the spring located on the site, called Government Spring, which had been used to supply water to Fort Brooke. A Native American tribe believed the water had healing properties and was a holy site on which tribes would not fight. This location helped to propagate the rumor embellished by explorers and Native Americans that the waters promoted youth and longevity. [31]

The Florida Brewing Company and **Ybor City Ice Works** at 5th Avenue and 13th Street, 1898, Tony Pizzo's Collection, USF Tampa Library, Special and Digital Collections. See Picture Index for license

On page 50, the building as it appears today. Note the faded **"FLORIDA BREWING CO."** on the side. *Below*, artist Terry Klaaren created a mural in the offices of the Swope, Rodante law firm in 2016 of the structure and its surrounding support buildings at the time of their construction.

Below, a widescreen of the bulding with flags, courtesy of the law firm Swope, Rodante, photographer Darrian Bagley.

Today in Tampa there are more than forty breweries of all types, including the craft breweries in Ybor City listed below, which continue the brewing tradition originally started by Ybor. In Ybor City there are a number of establishments serving craft beers. All those below have brewing operations. Some include restaurants or have food offerings in addition to beer. Some provide scheduled nightly music entertainment.

BarrieHaus Beer Co., 1403 E. 5th Avenue

Cigar City Cider and Mead, 1812 N. 15th Street

Coppertail Brewing Co., 2601 E. 2nd Avenue

Tampa Bay Brewing Company, 1600 E. 8th Avenue

Above, **marker outside the Florida Brewing Company** building now occupied by the Swope, Rodante law firm.

RESTAURANTS, BREWPUBS, CAFÉS, AND COFFEEHOUSES

Today in Ybor City, the establishments for good eating are unrivaled. With more than fifty restaurants and other eating places in the Historic District, dining can be found that will satisfy even the pickiest food critic. Some are historic operations like the *Columbia Restaurant* dating back to 1905, *Carmine's* dating from 1948, and *Bernini* from the 1970s. Their reputations for dining have been firmly established. Others are fairly new, like *7ᵗʰ + Grove* and the neighboring *Roast,* a deli and bakery; *Casa Santo Stefano,* with its Sicilian signature dishes; and *Flor Fina* and the *Café Quiquiriqui* in the boutique Hotel Haya. Even these relative newcomers have already made their marks.

The cafés and coffeehouses all compete for the smoothest, most flavorful café con leche, which is coffee with steamed milk, the strong but smooth Cuban coffee of Ybor. Coffee shops and cafés abound for the more casual diner. The cafés have their own individual character, whether it is *The Bricks* on the west end of Ybor, *Café Quiquiriqui* in Hotel Haya, or *La Creperia Cafe* where entrees and desserts are crepe-inspired. The hot beverage seeker can make the rounds to *The Bricks, King Corona Cigars, Pete's Ybor, The Foundation Coffee Co.,* the *Blind Tiger Cafe,* or *22ⁿᵈ Street Coffee* to find the perfect fit for an important routine in their day. Each is seeking to match a profile of a customer who will be a loyal patron. Menus are posted on the outside of most restaurants. The *Ybor City Pocket Guide,* in its e-book edition, lists

more than forty restaurants with links to their menus. Never has learning about what to eat in Ybor been easier.

Below, diners at the *Columbia Restaurant* experience one of its elegant dining rooms, as they eat chef-inspired dishes. The abundance of dining establishments means service and great food are a necessity for business success.

Ybor City Chamber of Commerce led by Lee Bell, President and CEO, provides a major leadership role in preserving and developing the historic district. *Above*, monthly luncheons of the Chamber take place in the Siboney Dining Room of the Columbia Restaurant. Courtesy of PamElla Lee Photography.

The **Roast** and *7th + Grove*, pictured *below,* are popular weekend destinations.

There are eateries like *GameTime* or *Gaspar's Grotto Pirate Bar & Restaurant*, which provide great options for children and are more American in their food offerings.

A number of restaurants serve deviled crab, a dish originating in Ybor City, which was easily served to the cigar workers at lunch from a vending wagon. The cigar workers ate the delicacy by holding it in their hands, but at *Carmine's* and elsewhere, a knife and fork will suffice for either of two sizes. As one *Carmine's* waiter noted, "you can order deviled crab the size of a chicken egg or the size of a dinosaur egg." Unlike the crab cakes of Boston or Baltimore, this crab dish is only breaded on the outside—leaving pure crab meat inside containing herbs and spices—before being deep fried. *Below,* eye catching pizza acrobat in the front window of Due Amici and Devil Crab at Carmine's.

At *Flor Fina* in the Hotel Haya, diners enjoy dishes that are a blend of the various Latin cuisines in Ybor, so an entrée can have Italian, Cuban, and Spanish characteristics. These dishes illustrate the influence of different immigrant groups who came to Ybor and contributed to the diversity and richness of the culture.

The brewpubs serve anything from American dishes like gourmet burgers, to old world shepherd's pie and beer-infused dishes at *Tampa Bay Brewing Company*. Several have restaurants and offer a beer-tasting sample of their craft beers, which are often brewed on-site.

While a number of restaurants have seafood offerings, *Shrimp & Co.* is devoted exclusively to this cuisine. There is an Indian restaurant, *Rasoi Indian Cuisine*; *El Puerto Restaurant & Grill* prepares South American dishes; and *Asiatic Steet Food + Noodle Bar* and *Samurai Blue* both serve Asian food. *Samurai Blue* is a sushi restaurant that serves a great steak as well. And then there is the popular *Acropolis Greek Taverna*. Southern style cooking can be found at *7th + Grove* and at *Al's Finger Licking Good Bar-B-Que* and *Al's Finger Licking Good Soul Food*.

There are hidden jewels whose uniqueness is a great attraction, such as the distinctive entrées at the Italian *La Terrazza Ristorante*, *Flor Fina at Hotel Haya*, the *Flan Factory* on Nebraska Avenue, and *Spook Easy Lounge.*.

For pizza lovers, Ybor has it whether you go to *Bernini*, *New York New York Pizza,* or *Due Amici* among others. Pizza with the freshest ingredients and signature combinations have been known to impress Ybor diners. The Italian restaurants represent this Latin group well. Italian immigrants provided the all-important food niche in the economy. Italian farmers cultivated the northern and eastern ends of the Ybor community and provided Italian grocers with their produce, which, in turn, made Ybor food-sustaining.

Some of the eating establishments offering Ybor's traditional Cuban sandwich include the *Columbia Restaurant, La Segunda Bakery, Carmine's, Gaspar's Grotto Pirate Bar & Restaurant* and *Tampa Bay Brewing Company*.

La Segunda Bakery

The historic bakery of Ybor City, established in 1915 and owned by the same family since its founding, makes Cuban bread that gets shipped out to points all over Florida and beyond every day. Its amazing prepared foods constitute a menu for takeout. Offerings range from substantial meals to sandwiches to bakery delicacies that include light and flaky guava pastries.

Below, the line frequently found inside the bakery is worth the wait. At *bottom*, the outdoor poster is by artist Tim Boatright, which features four items of comfort food for which Ybor City is famous. Courtesy of PamElla Photography.

VINTAGE SHOPS

★ ★ ★

Agora, located on E. 7th Avenue between 15th and 16th Streets, can best be characterized as an "old world store," providing heritage products from all over the world. Its contents are fascinating, and it is definitely worth a visit. Products include candles, colorful lamps, hemp products, textiles, jewelry, dishware, spices, herbal products, incense, soaps, minerals, crystals, and more.

Agora's front window on E. 7th Avenue. Courtesy of Agora.

Below is an interior picture showing **Agora's unique merchandise** of goods and furnishings for homes as well as businesses. Courtesy of Agora.

Agora—a word from the ancient Greeks meaning a space serving as an area for assembly and a place for commerce and social activities—lives up to its name.

The colorful products are eye- catching as the customer views the interesting collection of goods that can be found there.

Seekers of vintage fashion come from the rest of the nation to Ybor City to seek out La France, a vintage clothing store, located on E. 7th Avenue in Centro Ybor, *pictured above and below*, and within a few feet of Vicente Martinez-Ybor's bronze statue. The store features classical and retro styles for both men and women. Staff are available to assist shoppers with customized outfits and accessories from a large collection. Whether the style is for everyday, a special occasion, or a definitive look, visitors see an extensive offering of clothing options.

Jill Wax and son, Ben, stand behind the counter of **La France**, their vintage clothing store, established in 1974. Photos courtesy of La France.

For a historic district that went through its own life and near death transition, the longstanding Dysfunctional Grace shop in Tampa, is at home in Ybor City with its vintage life and death oddities. A bazaar of the strange and exotic for home décor or personal token, it is reminiscent of a Ripley's Believe It or Not. The shop both shocks the customer with its uniqueness and its depictions of the stages of life. The atmosphere appeals to all ages as a journey through the shop becomes one of discovery, mystery, and revelation.

Unique décor settings at Dysfunctional Grace. Courtesy of Liz Furlong.

While the Ybor City Chamber of Commerce Visitor Information Center on 8th Avenue in Centro Ybor is the first place to visit to determine how to plan your day, it also boasts a great gift shop. One-of-a-kind souvenirs feature everything about Ybor City. Beautiful cigar boxes, Spanish flamenco dolls, and mosaic roosters lay next to magnets featuring scenes of historic Ybor City. The shop carries a significant number of titles about Ybor City. Choose from unique candles made in Ybor City and a large assortment of T-shirts and caps. Many products are the work of local artists depicting various Ybor City scenes on notecards, postcards, and magnets alongside vintage cigar labels from the past, framed and unframed. Cigar boxes painted with Ybor City scenes by artist and historian Joe King Carter are an artistic highlight of items found in the gift shop.

The **gift shop's display of art books** by Dr. Ferdie Pacheco, who was born in Ybor City and painted numerous scenes of Ybor City and its social life.

Below, two of the T-shirt styles.

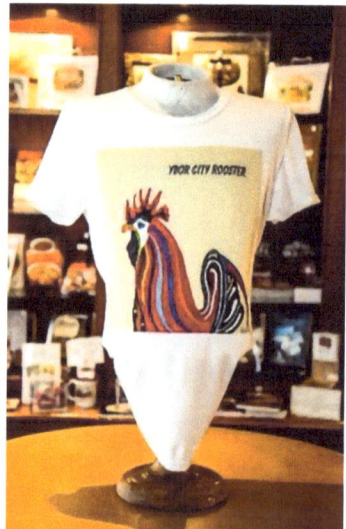

The **Columbia Restaurant Gift Shop**, with an entrance located at the corner of E. 7th Avenue and 21st Street, provides cookbooks of its signature dishes as well as food and cooking products used by the restaurant. It sells gift baskets in various arrangements featuring its popular items. The gift shop has a beautiful collection of Spanish pottery for sale. Gift cards are available, and some items may be purchased online. It's a popular place to visit either before or after dinner at the adjoining Columbia Restaurant. [32]

7th Avenue entrance to the **Columbia Restaurant Gift Shop** showing tile work.

OPEN-AIR MARKETS

Above, view of the **Ybor City Saturday Market** from 9th Avenue across from the Ybor City Museum State Park.

Ybor City is known for its street markets in the Historic District offering merchandise similar to that of a flea market but also including vintage items and antiques. The Ybor City Saturday Market, *above* and *next page*, fronts 8th Avenue between 18th and 19th Streets and attracts visitors from across the state. The market sells not only produce and prepared foods but also local crafts of every kind and description. Centennial Park is the home base of the chickens of Ybor City. The have called Ybor City home since they were brought by the original settlers. Now feral, they are displaced on Saturday when the park is pressure-washed before the market tents are set up. The chickens take to the streets and raise a fuss until the market disassembles and they can return to their home grounds.

Above, view of the **Ybor City Saturday Market** from 8th Avenue near the Centennial Park Streetcar Station.

Vintage Roost, *below*, is where vintage comes to roost just past the Columbia Restaurant off 7th Avenue at 23rd Street. It is a three-day, twice-a-month market, which features the creations of numerous vendors and many antiques. Artistic works are often one-of-a-kind, including remodeled furniture. Handmade items include creations for home décor, which are often seasonal. Abstract art has a presence as well as lamps from traditional table lamps to stained glass.

Left, **Vintage Roost Logo**.
Right, furnishing displayed under a warehouse roof at **Vintage Roost**. Images courtesy of Vintage Roost.

Stained Market Place is located in a warehouse on the north side of Ybor City on E. 15th Avenue. This densely packed warehouse of second hand items reflects a flea market with items ranging from Do It Yourself restoration projects, salvage and thrift to vintage and antiques. Local artists are supported and provide one-of-a-kind items at reasonable prices. Treasures for decorating rooms in a home or place of business are in the eyes of the avid seeker of a bargain.

Top, furnishings featured at the **Stained Market Place**. Images courtesy of Stained Market

Above, **Stained Market Place Logo**.

THE ARTS

The revitalization of Ybor City began in the 1970s and 1980s with an influx of artists who sought studio and living spaces among the remaining factory and retail buildings, then derelict in an Ybor City that was a community in decline. They created living and work areas by improving premises that property owners were all too willing to have occupied. The move of artists to Ybor City began with visual and performance art that included painters, craftspeople, artisans, musicians, poets, and writers. The vitality they brought to Ybor City attracted other businesses, including bars and nightclubs, and as old buildings were restored to meet these new purposes, property values increased, thereby making rent or ownership unaffordable for many artists.

A survivor from this early period is the collective of artists known as the Ybor Art Colony, made up of artists using a variety of materials for visual art, from the pencil to the brush, from portraiture to landscapes, from traditional impressionism to modern art. While its gallery and studios on the second floor above the King Corona Cigars are the artistic presence that never left, the studios are closed for building renovation and the collective is due to relocate. A valued center of the arts in Ybor is the Hillsborough Community College, Ybor Campus, Visual and Performing Arts program, a presence in the Ybor community dating back to the 1970s. The Performing Arts Building houses Gallery 114 and two theaters. An active schedule of performances including theater, concerts, and dance; and gallery exhibitions are a highlight for the community.

Above, street view of the **Kress Building**, courtesy of Dave Decker Photography.

In 2022, the arts community was joined by a new arts hub in the Kress Building, formerly occupied by the Kress five and dime store chain until the early 1980s. This new center has the Florida Museum of Photographic Arts occupying the first floor in 2023, fulfilling the vision for the building as a center for the arts. The second floor is a enclave of artists known as Kress Contemporary, which is space devoted to studios and galleries of visual, performing, and literary art. Members currently utilize studio space on the second and third floors of the Kress Building. Through a residency program for visiting artists, Tempus Projects, which curates award winning exhibitions, provides a place to stay while their work is on exhibit or their collaboration continues. The developing hub has been joined by the Tampa International Fringe Festival which brings a wide range of performing arts, including dramatic plays, improv, and shows for adults and children. The arts scene is another facet to the Ybor experience, where art, history, cuisine, entertainment, and shopping come together in its community for the public to enjoy. In this way Ybor celebrates the heritage of its past while seeking new claims on the future.

Giving to the Ybor Arts

Those who live, work, and visit Ybor City have the privilege of experiencing a local arts center in the Kress Building. The organizations and individuals housed there give the Ybor, Tampa community the opportunity to support the arts on a local level which brings the community together across the lines of age, race, ethnicity, and culture. Arts organizations only exist with the support of their communities. A strong arts presence stimulates tourism and exposure to the arts, which in turn benefits business. Local support allows donors including volunteers to see the benefits of their involvement directly. Through regular financial giving the continuity of an arts community can be achieved which helps talented and creative people make a living and provides for art education and appreciation of the arts for young people to adults.

Art in Ybor can be appreciated in many ways—attending live performances of musicians at various venues, inviting friends to art events and dinner in Ybor, like the flamenco performed at the Columbia Restaurant, taking in special events at Kress Contemporary, and viewing the numerous murals in Ybor City. For the dedicated work of artists displaying their creativity and talent, the appreciation goes both ways—to the grateful artist for the recognition of their work and to the person who identifies with the artist's unique creation.

Below, a drone shot of **Kress Contemporary**, courtesy of Dave Decker Photography.

VISUAL ARTS: REVERB | Ybor Art Factory | MERGECULTURE | OXH Gallery | Dave Decker Photography | Drift | Florida Museum of Photographic Arts | Gratus | Pop Yarn | Tempus Projects | Tempus Volta Artist Residency
PERFORMING ARTS: The Tampa Repertory Theater | The Fringe Theatre
LITERARY ARTS: Hear 'Em Say Youth Arts Collective | Kitchen Table Literary Arts

A GrowHouse poetry slam event. Courtesy of GrowHouse, Kress Contemporary

The Ybor community is a place where mainstream art forms and fringe alternatives create a new art scene that reflects a wide range of visual and performing arts. Diverse artistic expression where all creatives are equally respected further promotes the inclusivity of the Ybor community, where the contributions of each of its many mediums are accepted and appreciated.

Kress Contemporary Galleries

The galleries of Kress Contemporary provide a wide range of curatorial directives for visitors to explore. Here are the perspectives of a few.

REVERB serves as an extension of the University of South Florida College of Design, Art & Performance working in conjunction with Kress Contemporary. Its gallery provides an opportunity for artists and art historians to become an integral part of the art scene in Tampa. It is managed by graduate students with support from the USF's department.

The **Ybor Art Factory** provides exhibitions from a collective of Cuban artists which includes painting, drawing, sculpture, video art and object art as well as artistic installations representing contemporary Cuban art as it exists here and now.

MERGECULTURE is a gallery that focuses on the ways in which subcultures and countercultures in our society have contributed their own creativity as part of the art community's history and the extent to which they have been accepted and embraced by the art world.

Jenny Carey Studio/Gratus Gallery presents photographic, abstract images inspired by the transitions of the environment illustrating memory and loss. Tidal movements create their own etchings in the sand, which appear momentarily before being replaced by other abstract images created by water. A theme that runs through her works is the transitory and vulnerable nature of the environment which imprints a memory and then it is lost. jennycarey.com/

Tempus Projects is an arts nonprofit founded by Tracy Midulla that presents acclaimed exhibitions and artistic events within a wide range of visual expression. The nonprofit promotes emerging artists representing diverse cultural perspectives through exhibitions and collaborations. This effort is supported through an international artist residency program. Learn more about Tempus Projects and its ongoing exhibitions at tempus-projects.com

Tempus Projects has been the springboard for Kress Contemporary, nurturing and coordinating the Kress Arts scene on the eve of another enterprise. The Citrus Factory, for artist living and exhibition space in south Ybor, will solidify a 21st century diverse arts community joining those cultural societies established more than a century ago.

Drift is an ongoing exhibition series established by Tempus Projects dedicated to promoting and developing independent curators. It's a great place to get to know new and innovative artists and curators.

Tempus Volta, an initiative of the Tempus Projects community programs, provides project space for diverse artistic projects featuring small group shows and solo exhibits supporting individual exhibitions. Both emerging and established artists are supported.

Ghost Orchid: Fever Dream by Cristina Molina at Tempus Volta, courtesy of Tempus Projects.

Tampa Fringe

Fringe art refers to artistic expression that is not seen in curated art centers or classical style art festivals. Fringe stands for creative art expression that has not found a place in the theatre of performing arts or the exhibits of mainstream art galleries. There is a tremendous wealth of visual and performing art in the world that exists outside established centers of art. The Fringe celebrates these contributions of art expression placing a stamp of approval on what is attractive, meaningful, and appreciated by the public.

The Tampa International Fringe Festival

Tampa is part of the world's Fringe movement as it holds an International Fringe Festival every June for approximately 12 days. Kress Contemporary supports the Fringe art scene throughout the year and is the central venue for the Fringe Festival in Tampa. Fringe festivals are held annually throughout the world attracting huge attendance. Not only does Fringe honor visual arts with a wide range of mediums, but the performing arts are also well represented at the Tampa Festival and at Kress Contemporary throughout the year.

Tampa City Ballet

The Tampa City Ballet has a unique partnership with the Ybor City Historic District. The Ballet is supported by the Ybor City Redevelopment Area and is in partnership with the Florida Museum of Photographic Arts. The Ballet has performances annually at venues in Ybor City. The close ties of the ballet to Ybor City reinforce the cultural heritage of Ybor City with an organization that values the same social principles of diversity that made Ybor City a landmark community. The Tampa City Ballet seeks to give a deeper connection to its audiences through "innovative performances featuring original twenty-first century choreography…" Through its community educational programming for children, young adults, and those of retirement age, the Tampa City Ballet seeks to bring more people into the power of dance, into the dance of life itself for an ever-expanding audience for ballet.

Photo courtesy of Tampa City Ballet, Michael Sheehan, photographer.

The ballet has four major performances on an annual basis, some of which are free. The Tampa City Ballet distinguishes itself from other dance companies in many respects. It is a unique professional company of artists engaged in contemporary dance with a repertoire that is both groundbreaking and appeals to audiences across generational lines.

Photo courtesy of the Tampa City Ballet from the production of *7th Ave & Ybor*, the factory scene of cigar workers, courtesy of Soho Images and Tampa City Ballet, (Alicia Haselwood, Harlan Merhige).

Left, Len Bernstein, 2nd Avenue Deli, 1985, Gift of the Artist, FMoPA Permanent collection. *Right,* Bruce Dale, Title Unknown (Wigwam Hotel), c.1995, Gift of the Artist, FMoPA Permanent collection.

Florida Museum of Photographic Arts

Since 2001, the Florida Museum of Photographic Arts (FMoPA) has been showcasing exhibitions that have won critical acclaim for their contribution to capturing and reflecting culture. FMoPA collects, preserves and exhibits historic and contemporary works and is one of few such museums in the United States devoted solely to photography.

FMoPA exhibits span the evolution of photography from vintage to contemporary. The Museum's main gallery features rotating exhibits encompassing diverse genres and styles, ensuring a great experience with each visit. The FMoPA Community Gallery is dedicated to showcasing the Tampa Bay community and regularly features work from local photographers from its educational programs.

The Museum has a lengthy history of outreach and education to the Tampa Bay community by providing workshops and classes to children, adults, and seniors, demonstrating how photography can be used to inspire, educate and express.

FMoPA collaborates with neighboring art communities and galleries in an effort to create and facilitate an interconnected artistic ecosystem in Ybor. Its move to the first floor of the Kress Building in 2023 marked a major milestone in the new purpose of the building and established Ybor City as a nexus for the arts in Tampa and beyond. https://www.fmopa.org/

Hillsborough Community College Ybor City Arts

Visual and performing arts have been an important part of the curriculum of HCC Ybor City Campus since the school's founding. Its program centered in the Performing Arts building has brought continuity in the arts to the Ybor community for five decades. An emphasis on both the visual and performing arts is promoted through Gallery 114, its Mainstage theatre, and a smaller, more intimate theatre.

The school provides a high quality academic program of art instruction and development. Productions often involve bringing in talented professionals who work with students to develop impressive theatre experiences. The immersive environment in productions across the various departments from music, dance and visuals with students engaged in performing and working behind the scenes pro-

vide for a stimulating academic environment connected to the world. This translates into sensational theatre experiences for the public. Through theatre and visual arts, the themes of historic Ybor City are often featured. The active schedule of performing events including concerts, dance, and theatre productions as well as gallery exhibitions, are open to the public. These opportunities are instrumental in developing the talent of young artists in an academic environment. Support for the arts at the higher education level contributes to a more sustainable

arts community in Ybor. It reinforces the cultural vitality of a historic district. The opportunities for partnership in the arts between the historic district and the HCC Ybor Campus are unlimited. Photos courtesy of HCC Visual and Performing Arts Program.

Marcolina's Fine Arts Gallery

Emerging from the dynamic art scene of New York, Guillo Perez III and Marcolina Mercado-Perez bring a unique cultural influence to Ybor City. Guillo, who began his artistic journey in Ybor, was guided by renowned mentors like Theo Wucjik. Marcolina's Fine Arts Gallery includes art education geared toward culturally enriching the community through an Academy of the Arts. This program offers a rich spectrum of classes encompassing a wide range of disciplines: portraiture, sculpture, print making, and drawing. The comprehensive Academy of Arts occurs weekly providing a consistent and immersive experience.

Tai Chi classes offer a fresh approach in promoting creative inspiration. The critical exposure to art history is interwoven in Academy classes elevating the participants artistic journey and knowledge of their chosen mediums.

The gallery stands as the only space in the area to host nude life drawing sessions twice a month inviting artists and art enthusiasts alike to explore the nuances of the human form and enhance their skills. The gallery is also deeply engaged in the mural scene of Tampa Bay fostering a synergistic relationship with the community's vibrant street art culture.

Art enthusiasts may acquire artworks both online and at the gallery on 7th Avenue and at other affiliates found through their website at marcolinas.com. The gallery's collection spans a wide range of artistic mediums from the classical to the avant gard, promising a captivating and enriching artistic experience. It draws from the talents of the local community, the international sphere, and from contributions from their Academy of the Arts showcasing class creations.

Previous page, front window of **Marcolina's Fine Arts Gallery**, courtesy of the gallery. *Above,* an evening class, courtesy of the gallery.

Ybor Heritage Artists

Within the Ybor community are artists devoted to producing art that reflects the heritage of Ybor City and the life and times of its community. Some of these artists include the following:

Ferdie Pacheco (1927-2017)

Ferdie Pacheco was born in Ybor City and was a physician with a clinic in Miami where he was connected with boxing health and became the fight doctor for Muhammad Ali. He was also an artist who painted numerous scenes of the life and times of Ybor City where he lived. Some of his art is portrayed in the two books displayed *on the next page, Pacheco's Art of Ybor City* and *Pacheco's Art of the Cubans in Exile,* as well as in children's books. His colorfully vivid paintings project the life of Ybor City through street scenes and community settings. They document life through cafés, factories, restaurants, and street scenes at times of celebration.

Nancy Henderson

Nancy Henderson is renowned for her architectural drawings. They reflect the historic sites in Ybor City in both ink and pen with color and are also rendered in ink and pen only. Her sketches can be beautifully framed and are available on her website. Notecard editions of her works are available in the Ybor City Chamber of Commerce Visitor Information Center. See the ink sketch of the casitas by Nancy Henderson under the section Architecture, which follows.

Arnold Martinez (1931-2021)

Arnold Martinez's paintings of Ybor's heritage include the use of ingredients not otherwise used in the art world for paint. He has painted with Cuban coffee, tobacco, and tea, often blended together into various shades and tones in his depiction of Ybor scenes and landmarks. His gallery in Ybor City was a great place to meet the artist and view his works.

Joe King Carter and David Audet

Artist Joe King Carter, a long-term resident of Ybor City and community activist for many years, has conveyed the heritage of Ybor City through the numerous interviews he has given. Through his artwork and walking tours, he continues to promote the heritage of the community. Central to Ybor City's murals is the one entitled Tampa Town, formerly on exhibit at King Corona Cigars. It is being relocated to a more public space. Carter, along with David Audet, another long-term resident artist who joined with Carter to create *Tampa Town* mural, are engaged in a new mural project at

La France, a 7th Avenue clothing store for men and women. The *Tampa Town* mural depicts dozens of smaller scenes of people interacting, all reflecting the life and times of Ybor City. See the mural he and David Audet created on the following pages. *Below* are two Carter paintings reflecting the street life of Ybor. Courtesy of the artist.

Ron Watson

Ron Watson's drawings, encompassing many portraits, is best described by the term "shades of gray," referring to the extensive range of gray used with his graphite pencil to render incredibly lifelike results. He is a trained artist and has taught art at the college level. He has created numerous portraits of famous historic figures of Ybor City, including Don Vicente Martinez-Ybor, Eduardo Manrara, and Pauline Pedroso. His portraits also reveal the faces of important leaders of the Cuban independence movement that are not as well known, but which reflect that there were numerous leaders of the independence movement that have not been recognized by history.

Left, **Paulina Pedroso**, Afro Cuban leader of the Cuban Independence movement in Ybor City.
Right, **Don Vicente Martinez-Ybor**, next to a portrait of **Eduardo Manrara**. Courtesy of the artist.

FLAMENCO

The Spanish art form of flamenco permeates the experience of Ybor City and no introduction to the culture is complete without it. Through music, song, and dance, the performers express a wide range of emotions, which can penetrate deep inside the observer, creating a personal experience. It is a genre that continues to evolve and requires intensive training and physical fitness for those dedicated to this expressive art form. The Tampa Bay Flamenco Dance Company is performing in its fourth decade at the Columbia Restaurant with performances six days a week. The shows require a reservation for dinner and the show. The dance company also provides lessons for all levels of students from beginners to advanced. [34] The dancers are a main attraction at the Ybor Chamber of Commerce's Fiesta Day held annually in February. The dance company performs at various venues in the Tampa area.

Below, **Maria Esparza**, artistic dance director for the Tampa Bay Flamenco Dance Company, strikes a pose in the troupe's dressing room prior to taking the stage.

Above, the **Tampa Bay Flamenco Dance Company** performing at the Columbia Restaurant. *Below*, a formal picture of the **Tampa Bay Flamenco Dance Company** on the balcony of the El Patio Room of the Columbia Restaurant. Photos courtesy of the Dance Company.

MURALS

Tampa has many murals throughout the city. The ones in Ybor City are particularly noteworthy. Outside murals come and go due to the elements which degrade the work of art, and to building restoration and other construction. *Below* is the original ***Viva Ybor*** mural painted by Chico Garcia in 2012, at 7th Avenue between 19th and 20th Streets. It depicts some of the major icons of Ybor City's history. [35] From the left is the Ybor City rooster and hen who enjoy protected legal status according to city ordinance and have the right of way for vehicular traffic. Their avian ancestors made their way from Spain to Cuba to Key West, then to Tampa as they provided a valuable source of food on the hoof in the late nineteenth century before refrigeration. At the bottom left is the tombstone of the famous rooster, James E. Rooster, a remarkably beautiful rooster who was buried in Ybor City in 1997 amid a New Orleans-style funeral procession featuring brass instruments.

Previous mural 2012. Image published under commercial license from Picfair.com.

The iconic lamppost of Ybor is positioned above the rooster. Its five enormous bulbs illuminated the streets of Ybor first as lit lamps, then gas, then electric, inadvertently representing the five major cultural and ethnic groups of Ybor—Spaniards, Cubans, Italians, Romanians, and Germans. Through the upper middle of the mural is Henry B. Plant's Tampa Bay Hotel with its exotic onion-shaped minarets and rounded cupolas of Moorish architecture, which was popular during the Victorian era. Below the Tampa Bay Hotel (now the Henry B. Plant Museum on the University of Tampa campus) is the yellow streetcar. In front of the streetcar is the logo of the Hav-A-Tampa Cigar Company, which moved to the Dominican Republic in 2009. Overlooking the scene in the upper right is a very serious Vicente Martinez-Ybor who arrived in Tampa to start his new enterprise at age sixty-eight and oversaw its first ten years of development until his death in 1896.

The **current mural**, pictured *below*, contains many of the same symbols and images, with the insertion of the American flag and the flags of Cuba and Puerto Rico on the sides (not shown). A pirate brandishing a sword is a nod to the Gasparilla Festival. [36]

The Arrival of the Spanish Expedition is a tile mural installed during the Columbia Restaurant's stewardship under Cesar Gonzmart. On the exterior of the restaurant, it commemorates the arrival of the Spanish Expedition funded by King Ferdinand and Queen Isabella of Spain that discovered America believing it was the West Indies. [37]

The artists of the *Tampa Town* **mural**, Joe King Carter and David Audet

The *Tampa Town* mural (2013) contains many separate scenes of life in Ybor City that are melded together in this diorama created by David Audet and Joe King Carter. It is a mash-up of people (both fictional and real) and places throughout Tampa, with an emphasis on Ybor City. The artwork is acrylic on wood, eight feet by eleven feet, an homage to New York artist Red Grooms. Created for an artists' and writers' group event, The Cuban Sandwich Show, it was previously on display at King Corona Cigars and is being relocated to a more public space in Ybor City. Photo of mural by Dave Decker Photography, courtesy of artists David Audet and Joe King Carter. [38]

The ***1937 Antifascist Women's March* mural**, *above*, is located on the west side of the building located at 2015 E. 7th Avenue. It features the leaders of the march in Tampa and activists who led political opposition to the brutal fascist movement in Spain and elsewhere in the 1930s. The phrase "no pasarán" means "they shall not pass," a reference to the slogan of the democratic forces that held their positions in the Spanish Civil War to impede the progress of fascist forces from moving past their lines. The mural depicts three women. Dolores Ibárruri Gómez, on the left, was a Spanish antifascist activist who was a leader of the movement abroad. In the middle is Luisa Moreno and on the right is Margot Falcón Blanco. Both were activists in Tampa advocating for labor and women's rights, as well as opposing fascism, and were leaders of the demonstration. The local artist is Michelle Sawyer.

The mural and marker are an important stop on the trail of understanding Ybor City and what brought immigrants to America, a place where they would have the freedom to follow their aspirations. The mural was commissioned by historian Sarah McNamara, who authored *Ybor City: Crucible of the Latina South*, released in 2023. The book includes a chapter about the Antifascist Women's March of 1937 in which McNamara's aunt, Margot Falcón Blanco, was a march organizer. The mural and historical marker were dedicated to the memory of those who participated in the march. [39]

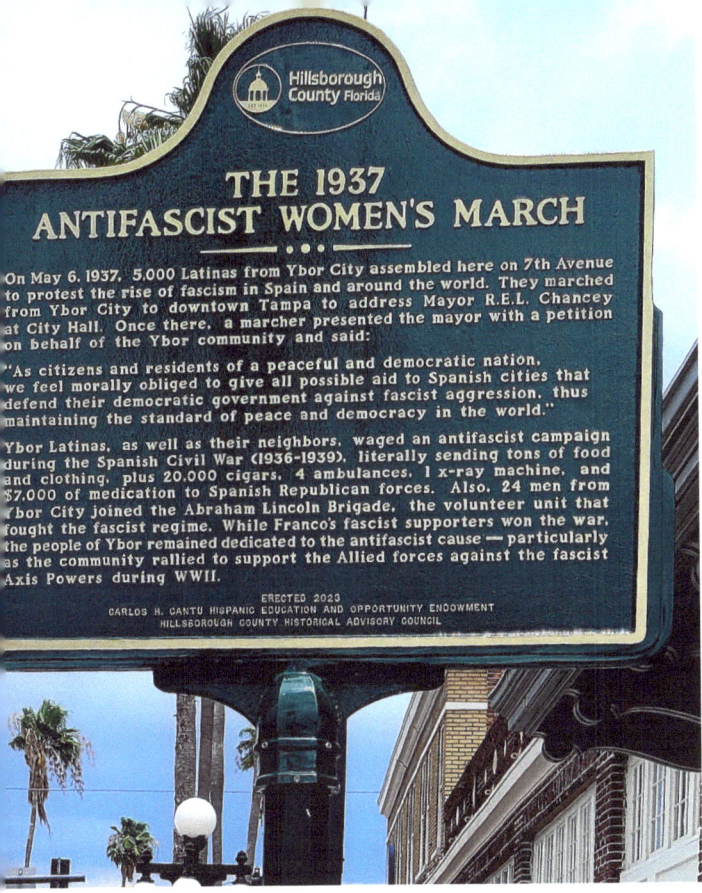

Left, front / west side of **1937 Antifascist Women's March marker** located on E. 7th Avenue. [40]

Right, reverse / east side of marker.

The mural, *below*, on the west side of the Sociedad La Union Martí-Maceo building is not viewable due to construction and the impact of the elements, but pictorial representations can depict the artist's work. The mural depicts the Afro Cuban community's cultural history and some of the historical symbols and icons of the group.

The flag of Cuba, which was to be the national flag of the new Cuban nation, flies to the right of a lector, atop a cigar factory building which occupies the central feature of the mural. The mural depicts scenes of Ybor in the 1920s, showing cars, streetcars, and architecture of the time. The mustached individual on the left of the trio of pictures is José Martí, who recognized that the support of the Afro Cuban community would be essential if the independence of Cuba was to be achieved.

Above José Marti is the portrait of Paulina Pedroso, and to the right of José Martí is the image of Afro Cuban General Antonio Maceo, who led the largest contingent of troops in the final push for independence in 1895, consisting primarily of Afro Cubans.

Through the mural is a vine that is occasionally wrapped around a cowrie shell, which in African spiritual life was a symbol of protection and prosperity. The shell represents the strength and constancy of the ocean and the faith that life requires.

Martí-Maceo mural, Historic Ybor City on the Sociedad La Union Martí-Maceo building. Contributor RKG, South Florida/picfair.com. Used under commercial license. [41] City of Tampa Mural Collection, Artist: Derick Washington, Title: *Wall of Martinez*.

Pictured *below*, in the Roosevelt Room at Hotel Haya resides an oil-on-canvas painting of Theodore Roosevelt entitled ***The Charge of the Yellow Rice Brigade***. The line refers to the traditional story of the arrival of Lt. Colonel Teddy Roosevelt and his "Rough Riders" (a nickname for the first US Volunteers Cavalry Regiment) in Ybor City. In early June 1898, the troops descended in masse upon a café known as Las Novedades, once housed in the property adjacent to the hotel, and now owned by it, at 7th Avenue and 15th Street. The troops were enthusiastically welcomed by the local population and were served the well-known Cuban dish of yellow rice and chicken. The event is humorously referred to as the opening salvo in the brigade's involvement in the Spanish-American War. In the mural, Teddy Roosevelt sits on his horse, Texas, who along with his dog, Cuba, accompanied him to Cuba. Also pictured are two other mascots of the Rough Riders, a golden eagle and a mountain lion cub. Following their arrival, many of the troops encamped on the eastern side of Ybor in the vicinity of what would later be the site of the Columbia Restaurant. Within weeks of the troops' arrival, the invasion flotilla disembarked from Port Tampa to the war that would last approximately three months and free Cuba from Spanish control. [42]

Mural of Teddy Roosevelt in the Roosevelt Room of Hotel Haya.

THE CHARGE OF THE YELLOW RICE BRIGADE

Google Earth image photo of the *American Journey* mural.

Above, the **American Journey mural** on Adamo Drive between 17th and 19th Streets was created under the direction of Michael Parker, who utilized students from Ybor City's Hillsborough Community College. The project involved extensive planning, funding, and preparation of the two-block metal warehouse surface. The mural has multiple themes: "The Journey through Life," "The Conflict between Tradition and Progress," and "The American Experience." Featured in the mural are Don Vicente Martinez-Ybor, Dr. Frank Adamo, inventor of an innovative treatment using hydrogen peroxide, and Tampa historian Tony P. Pizzo. The surface of the work is corrugated metal of a warehouse, occupying 12,000 square feet. The mural is the largest outdoor work of art in Florida. [43]

Below, on the campus of Hillsborough Community College, Ybor, are two murals reflecting the heritage of the Ybor community in which the school is embedded. The **Living Shades** mural is located on the east side of the Ybor Campus Visual Arts Building on 11th Avenue and spans the length of the building. It was created by artists Jay Giroux and Edgar Sanchez Cumbas. The vibrantly colorful mural contains many symbols and representations of the Historic District.

Image courtesy of HCC Ybor, Department of Visual and Performance Arts. [44] https://www.hccfl.edu/campus-life/arts/galleries-hcc/grounds4art, *below*.

A second heritage mural located on the HCC Ybor campus entitled **Generations** by artist Trinity Rivard is located in the bi-level passageway between the campus's Ybor Building and the Faculty Building off 9th Avenue. The mural reflects the generations of immigrants who have lived and worked in the Ybor neighborhood. It blends the history of Ybor with the vital presence of the school in the Historic District. The mural is a creation of faculty and students at HCC Ybor executing the design of Rivard.

Below and on the *next* page, *Generations* mural, courtesy of HCC Ybor, Department of Visual and Performance Arts. [45]

ARCHITECTURE

With a Historic District that encompasses more than seven cultural and ethnic groups in a single community, a unique characteristic of Ybor City is its varied architecture. The casitas, small houses, were uniquely built to withstand living in what was initially a hostile environment. On the *next page* are further examples of the varied architectural features found in Ybor City.

A shophouse—a store on the first floor with living quarters on the second floor—is shown in the two images below. Often referred to generally in American parlance as "mixed-use" or "dual-use," the structure can best be described by the oriental terms "shophouse" or "houseshop." It existed in New Orleans and is believed to have been brought to Ybor City's 7th Avenue by immigrants from its older sister city on the Gulf. The architectural features resemble the New Orleans French Quarter with wrought-iron balconies overhanging the shop below, which compensated for lack of a backyard. The term has been shortened in the twentieth century to "shouse" or "shome." This age-old architectural feature dates back to the Middle Ages in both Europe and the Far East. The shophouse construction in Ybor City took advantage of 7th Avenue's central location to commercial activity. [46].

Chill Bros. Scoop Shop and adjacent businesses, *below right,* reflect the house-shop feature of construction that allowed for frontage of many businesses on famed 7th Avenue.

The Long Ash Cigar Shop and the adjacent Due Amici restaurant, *below left,* share a similar shophouse façade of a wrought-iron balcony overhanging their businesses on 7th Avenue.

Above, **sketch of casitas** by Nancy Henderson. Used with permission.

The casitas were built by Vicente Martinez-Ybor and his colleagues, who owned cigar factories, for their cigar workers. Thousands of these structures were built beginning in 1886. A Casita Tour originates from the Ybor City Museum State Park.

The Castle, *below* and *right*, originally the Labor Temple, dates back to 1930. It was built as a hall for various unions serving the cigar industry. The building has a Norman Tower modified by Renaissance features and serves as a popular nightclub referred to as "The Castle."

The Castle Nightclub, 9th Avenue and 16th Street. Its **Norman Tower** at *right*.

The Italian Club, east side on 18th Street, showing the heavy plastered features of its window frames and cartouche.

The stately Italian Club, L'Unione Italiana (1918), seen *above* from its eastern 18th Street side, on 7th Avenue was designed by architects Malachi Leo Elliott and Bayard Clayton Bonfoey, who were also architects of the Circulo Cubano de Tampa and the Centro Asturiano de Tampa. [47] The building incorporates the Italian Renaissance style with its heavy masonry framed windows. The imposing building shown is accented with marble and rounded Greek columns with Corinthian capitals. Above the second-floor windows are cartouches, a style introduced during the French Renaissance; they are unique to the building. The cartouche, which depicts an oculus, a round eye-like disc, represents the theme of the building, looking ahead to the future, and is supported on either side by a cornucopia representing the abundant life of the move to America. The cartouche, which in Egyptian hieroglyphics was a symbol that identified a name, was brought into French usage during the time when Napoleon was in Egypt and adopted into French architectural design.

The Cuban Club, El Circulo Cubano de Tampa (1917), *below*, designed by M. Leo Elliott, presents an architectural style that is neo-Greek-Classical with two heavy Greek columns with Corinthian capitals and has a Greek classical triangular pediment with a balustrade to complete the roof line. This is the second building on this site, the previous building destroyed by fire. The long northern side fronting Palm Avenue resembles the façade of a palazzo with its symmetrical design, which encompasses the ballroom. [48]

El Centro Espanol de Tampa, National Park Service, P.D.

The Spanish Club, Centro Español de Tampa (1912), *above*, on 7th Avenue at 16th Street, was established in 1891 and is the second building on the site. It incorporates a variety of European styles. It reflects neo-French-Renaissance style which was a departure from the classical Greek and Gothic features. A Moorish influence is evident by its 7th Avenue entryway with alternating redbrick and white stone design and wrought-iron trim, which is utilized in the rest of the building's ornamentation as well. This adds another style to Ybor's panoply of architecture. The building currently houses restaurants. [49]

El Pasaje, The Cherokee Club (1886), *top of next page*, means "passageway" in Spanish and refers to the columns that line the front of the building. The two-story structure was the office building of Vicente Martinez-Ybor and one of the first brick buildings in Ybor City. Located on 9th Avenue at 14th Street, it is across the street from Vicente Martinez-Ybor's factory complex. Its design falls into the Italian Renaissance category with the outward rounded archway and columns common to Italian villa design.

The columns comprised of rounded redbrick laid against a solid column are a unique design element of the late nineteenth century. Ybor used the building to house important guests, including José Martí on the occasion of his first visit in 1891. Following Ybor's death, the building has been used for multiple purposes. It is also known as the Cherokee Club, which was a gentleman's club that occupied the space. It has also served as a hotel that served famous visitors, including Winston Churchill as a war correspondent during the Spanish-American War, as well as Lt. Colonel Theodore Roosevelt. It later became a restaurant, then a clinic. It is currently occupied by an energy company. [50]

El Centro Asturiano de Tampa (1914), *below,* formed in 1902 from an extension of Centro Asturiano de La Habana to support the Spanish immigrants from Asturias, is still active today. The style of the building is Renaissance Mediterranean with influence from those areas of the Northern Mediterranean: Spain, Italy, France, and Greece. The Greek columns bear a Doric capital. Between its massive windows is a cartouche, a French architectural feature which is of unique design to the building. [51]

The German American Club (1909), *below*, on Nebraska Avenue at 11th Street, resembles the simpler utilitarian lines of the French Directorate period and the early American Federalist period. Without elaborate features of earlier ornamental European architecture, its elegance is marked by its symmetry, accented with stone. [52]

The front entrance to the **Columbia Restaurant** with the loggias ending just short of the entrance protecting diners from inclement weather is stucco accented with colorful tile imported from Spain.

The freestanding archway, *below*, heralds the **entrance from Tampa proper into Ybor City**, the city's Fourth Ward at the Nuccio Parkway entrance to 7th Avenue. The street is one of America's most famous streets and is also referred to by locals as La Sétima. The archway is on the list of the world's freestanding archways. [53]. Courtesy of Cooper Johnson Smith Peterson, Architects & Town Planners.

Casa Santo Stefano, *below*, featuring Sicilian cuisine recognizes the influence of those who came to Ybor from Santo Stephano in central Sicily. Shown with its Italian villa features and garden at the drive-in-pick-up entrance.

FESTIVALS AND PARADES

Annual festivals and parades are a part of the life of Ybor City, in celebration of Tampa's diverse heritage characterized by the numerous immigrant groups who settled here. **JANUARY** events include the **Children's Gasparilla Parade**, occurring in late January along Bayshore Boulevard, featuring the Preschoolers' Stroll. It is followed a week later by the **Gasparilla Pirate Fest and Parade of Pirates**, who arrive in a seventeenth-century-period pirate ship to compel the mayor of Tampa to give them the keys to the city refused by the mayor the week before. The pirates land on a Saturday near the end of January, invading Tampa and parading to the mayor's office and throughout the city, disrupting the business operations and the population of Tampa. They depart the following week.

Left, **Gasparilla pirate invasion**, courtesy of Dave Decker Photography.

Right, **pirate ship invasion crew**, courtesy of Dave Decker Photography.

FEBRUARY events include **the Ybor City Chamber of Commerce's Fiesta Day and Promenade of Flags**, which occurs in late February. Vendors line 7th Avenue with vintage goods and prepared foods. The event celebrates the various cultures of Ybor City with cultural entertainment. The Promenade of Flags signifies all the nationalities whose peoples have come to be part of the United States.

Below, members of the **Tampa Bay Flamenco Dance Group performing on Fiesta Day** at Centro Ybor, courtesy of the dance group.

Also in February is the **Sant' Yago Knight Parade**, *below,* presented by the Krewe of the Knights of Sant' Yago. Other Krewes participate in the parade with marching bands, floats, and local political and social leaders of Tampa and Ybor City, Courtesy of Keir Magoulas, Visit Tampa Bay.

MARCH is the month of the **Tampa Pride Festival and Diversity Parade in Ybor City**. It includes an arts and crafts show, a community health fair, and features entertainment promoted by the Hillsborough Community College, Ybor Campus. Vendors are usually in the vicinity of the Cuban Club. A nightly concert takes place until eleven o'clock. Ybor City welcomes this community into the life and work of the city as it did numerous groups of immigrants, displaying its vision of acceptance and support for all who come to celebrate the uniqueness and contributions of their individual communities.

Photo *below* courtesy of Keir Magoulas, Visit Tampa Bay.

Also in March is the annual **Rough Riders St. Patrick's Night Parade**, which occurs on an evening close to St. Patrick's Day. It is led by the 1st US Volunteer Cavalry Regiment, the Rough Riders, whose mission is to promote their heritage and the contributions and accomplishments of Teddy Roosevelt and the members of the 1st US Volunteer Cavalry Regiment involved in the US victory in the Spanish-American War.

MAY is a busy month in Ybor. At the beginning of the month is **J.C. Newman Cigar Co. Founders Day**. The event is located on the campus of the J.C. Newman

Cigar Factory at 16th Street and Columbus Drive, and takes place on the first weekend of the month. Admission, tours of the facility, and games are all free. Food trucks sustain the crowd throughout the four-hour lunchtime event.

May is also becoming the month for the **Fringe Festival**, which occurs in Ybor City over a several-day period. The Tampa Fringe Festival was founded in 2016 to promote the creative freedom of the performing arts. There, you will see things that may not be found among the museums and exhibits of the traditional art world. Its theme is inclusivity as it celebrates the performing arts through dramatic skits and short plays that create a new avenue for artistic expression. The festival exists at multiple city venues with numerous special events showcasing all forms of art expression. The historic Kress Building is fringe central for the event. https://festival.tampafringe.org/

On Memorial Day weekend is the **International Cuban Sandwich Festival**, which occurs in Centennial Park from eleven to six. Vendors participate in making their best Cuban sandwiches to compete for Best Sandwich Award. Each year the sandwich makers participate in an attempt to create the largest Cuban sandwich in the world. Attendees get to identify for themselves their favorite Cuban sandwich at the many food booths at this event.

Below left, **the International Cuban Sandwich Festival** at Centennial Park, looking west on 9th Avenue in front of the Ybor City Museum, courtesy of CubanSandwich Festival.com.

Below right, An authentic **Cuban Sandwich** may be found at Hotel Haya's Café QuiquiRiqui and Flor Fina.

NOVEMBER kicks off in the middle of the month with the **Ybor City Chamber of Commerce Tree Lighting Ceremony** in Centro Ybor. The evening event is marked by entertainment from many groups from young children to adult choirs. Hot chocolate and cookies are served to the mass of attendees while they last. Centro Ybor on 7th Avenue at 16th Street is the staging point for the Ybor City Chamber's Tree Lighting, which begins the Christmas season in Ybor City.

Above, **Ybor City Chamber of Commerce Tree Lighting** in Centro Ybor, courtesy of Michael A. Murphy.

DECEMBER closes out the year with a **New Year's Eve Parade and Pep Rally** the day before the Tampa Bay Bowl, referred to beginning in 2023 as the ReliaQuest Bowl. *Below,* high school bands in Florida perform along with the two college bands from the schools who play in the bowl game. The night parade moves down 7th Avenue from 20th Street to 14th Steet before ending with a pep rally creating enthusiasm for the next day's game on New Year's Day.

Below left, the crew serving hot chocolate and cookies at the **Tree Lighting** huddle together, exhausted but smiling, as they have survived another year.

Below right, **New Year's Eve Parade**, courtesy of PamElla Lee Photography.

On the evening of the Lighting of the Tree 2023, a double rainbow precedes the first public event in Ybor City following a tragic October.

YBOR CITY FOR CHILDREN

★ ★ ★

There are many opportunities for children to experience and appreciate Ybor City. The **Ybor City Museum State Park** and the **Tampa Baseball Museum at the Al Lopez House** are small and manageable experiences for children and are located on the 9th Avenue side of Centennial Park. The Ybor City Museum depicts the history of Ybor through various media including audio, video, pictures, and written exhibits. The museum offers a tour of a neighboring casita, which reveals how people lived back in the late nineteenth and early twentieth centuries in Tampa. The Tampa Baseball Museum reveals the integral nature of the sport in the life of Ybor City and Tampa from the late 1800s through the present, detailing the achievements of many of baseball's great players from this area.

Interactive display of Al Lopez Field, courtesy of Arminda Mata, President & CEO of the Ybor City Museum Society.

Centennial Park, in the center of Ybor City, was dedicated at the centennial celebration in Ybor City in 1986. It features a statue, commissioned by Steven Dickey, of a family of immigrants—a father, mother, and two children as they arrive in Ybor City having embarked on a long journey from Europe. Statues of Anthony "Tony" P. Pizzo, Ybor historian, and Nick C. Nuccio, an Italian mayor of Tampa, are nearby. The park is the setting for the weekly Saturday Market, a marvel for both adults and children. During the week the park is the territory of many of Ybor's roosters. Hens with their chicks can be seen twice a year, in the spring and fall. A rare all-white rooster or one with many tail-feather colors is a chance for a great picture!

Many children and school groups attend the **Ybor City Historic Walking Tours.** They hear about the heroes of Ybor City, particularly Don Vicente Martinez-Ybor, José Martí, and others as shown at the **Friends of José Martí Park**, *above*. Courtesy of Ybor City Walking Tours.

Food stops and breaks have an important place in a visit to Ybor. **GameTime**, *above*, with its interactive games and kid-friendly food, is a great rest stop, as is Gaspar's Grotto Pirate Bar & Restaurant—Ybor's take on the Gasparilla Festival replete with pirate servers and food pleasing to all ages. Pizza places abound in Ybor as the appetite for this Italian staple can be enjoyed at New York New York Pizza, Bernini, and Due Amici, all on 7th Avenue.

Souvenir shopping and a plan for how to spend the day is provided by the Ybor City Chamber of Commerce **Visitor Information Center (the VIC)**, *right*, where exhibits of Ybor history can be explored and a short seven-minute orientation video can be viewed. The visit can be marked by the purchase of a special souvenir.

The **streetcar** is free with its four stops in Ybor City and seven more in Tampa proper. This public transportation can take children and adults alike to places like the Florida Aquarium, the American Victory Ship & Museum, Sparkman Wharf, the Tampa Riverwalk, and the Tampa Bay History Center. Not far beyond the last stop is the Glazer Children's Museum, the Tampa Museum of Art, and the Henry B. Plant Museum.

Below, **a streetcar pulls into Centro Ybor station**. The Spanish Club building is in the center and to its right is the VIC.

Stop 1, Centennial Park (The Ybor City Museum State Park and the Tampa Baseball Museum)

Stop 2, Centro Ybor (the VIC)

Stop 3, Streetcar Society (Hotel Haya and the Ybor Factory complex)

Stop 4, Cadrecha (José Martí Park, Noriega/Palm Parking Garage)

DRIP Ybor, "Do Really Inspirational Projects," is a new art environment for people of all ages. Its customers can learn and create in an establishment for people who want to express themselves in many mediums, including pottery, mosaics, and apparel design, with materials and guidance from staff. This new avenue allows for creative expression for all in a medium they feel comfortable working in. This establishment is great for kids and families and offers two locations on 7th Avenue, 1620 and 1910 E. 7th Avenue. https://drip-ybor.com/

Scenes from DRIP Ybor: *Top left*, a class in pottery making with instructor Jonathan Scanlon, aka Johnny Drip; *top right*, a honey pot mug creation; *below left*, a coiled pot & parrot; *below right*, clothing as a medium. Courtesy of DRIP Ybor.

Dysfunctional Grace Art Co., located on E. 7th Avenue, is a gallery of both art and merchandise that appeals to the interests of adults and children. Its theme focuses on the nature of life and death with exotic and unique items ranging from taxidermy to unique home furnishings or just a personal token. Photo used with permission. https://www.dysfunctionalgrace.shop/

SYMBOLS OF YBOR CITY

★ ★ ★

There are features of Ybor City that stand out as having successfully spanned its history from the very beginning to the present.

BRICK STREETS

The paving of streets with brick began in earnest in the first decade of the twentieth century. Bricks came from companies in the Southeast, especially Augusta, Georgia. The names of the foundries are often stamped on the bricks. *Right*, the intersection of 9th Avenue and 17th Street in front of the Hilton Garden Inn shows a brick pattern—a patchwork quilt of repairs keeping the streets usable.

STREETLAMPS

Historian Wallace Reyes, PhD, records that the first streetlamps came from New Orleans in 1887. [54] More lamps appeared on Ybor City streets when the city was designated as a landmark historic district in the early 1990s.

Rooster, hen, and chicks in the parking lot of the Hilton Garden Inn and just about everywhere else.

Chickens were introduced to Ybor City by the first cigar-worker settlers. They were brought to the Western Hemisphere by the Spanish when they arrived at the end of the fifteenth century in the Caribbean. Chickens made their way to Tampa by way of Cuba and Key West. Due to years of breeding on their own when Ybor City was in decline and the fowl were left to scratch for themselves, some have developed a rainbow of tail-feather colors. Protected by law, the chicken residents breed chicks in the spring and fall.

STREETCAR

The streetcar system has been a major influence in the development of Tampa's urban area. The streetcar line between Tampa and Ybor City was initially developed by Ybor. The cars are being redesigned to improve their ADA access. A more modern version is in the works.

Below, **streetcar** departing Centro Ybor station going west.

THE CASITAS

The Ybor City casita takes its place among other American housing designs like the bungalow, craftsman, and cottage structures. Modern editions of the house are being built in Ybor City and in Tampa. Today, restored casitas also provide accommodations for vacation rentals.

WHERE ALL ARE WELCOME

For more than 135 years, Ybor City has been a community where all are welcome. For the Spanish, Cubans, Afro Cubans, Italians, Sicilians, Germans, Romanians, and Eastern European Jews who came to Tampa, there were no separate neighborhoods. Afro Cuban cigar workers and their White Cuban colleagues mixed in Cuba and initially in Ybor City until US segregation laws required their separation and reinforced racism. They all lived and worked, relaxed, ate, and socialized in one community, one neighborhood, Ybor City. Each group had its own niche in the cigar economy. Well-educated Spanish lectors read from English literature and American newspapers, translating into Castilian Spanish as they read. Cubans and Afro Cubans were the bulk of cigar workers, including the cigar rollers who, at their peak of production, hand-rolled 500 million cigars in 1929. The Italians, who were primarily from Sicily, were farmers and grocers. They farmed land to the north and east of Ybor City and supplied their fellow Italian grocers with produce, allowing for a food-sustaining community. The Romanians and Jews were merchants who established dry good stores that sold furnishings, clothing, hardware, and other products. Germans were engaged in factories producing wooden cigar boxes, as well as printing and developing along with cigar factory owners, brilliantly colored cigar labels and cigar bands, which allowed for the industry to successfully promote its many brands. Whether the Ybor community was developing, booming, or declining, there was a unity and inclusiveness in its diversity.

In one place was a multilingual, multiethnic, multiracial immigrant environment composed of different religions. Today, the Historic District is as welcoming to all as it has always been. It is a place where all human beings are welcomed and accepted. This Historic District has LGBTQ+ owned businesses supported by other businesses who demonstrate their support for this community. The image above, *on the left*, displays the flags of the nationalities of those who emigrated to Ybor City. It is a seal created by the historian Anthony Pizzo. The flag on the right is the Progress Pride Flag, designed by Daniel Quasar, an inclusive symbol with five new colors shaped into an arrow pointing to the right, representing trans people, LGBTQ+ communities of color, and those affected by or have died from AIDS.

The five globe lamppost inadvertently represents the five major groups who immigrated to Tampa: Spanish, Cubans (Hispanic and Afro), Italians-Sicilians, Germans, and Romanians - one lamp, one community, Ybor City. Courtesy of Keir Magoulas, Visit Tampa Bay

JUST BEYOND YBOR

Just beyond Ybor City within two-and-a-half miles to the south and west are numerous opportunities to enjoy Tampa and the amazing Tampa Bay estuary. Many of these locations are along the streetcar line or within close proximity. See map at the end of this section. These sites include:

1- **The Florida Aquarium**, one of the best aquariums in the US, promoting conservation and protection of species with tours featuring the Tampa Bay estuary and the thousands of species which inhabit it. Scuba dive in a fish tank while you're there!

2- **American Victory Ship & Museum**, one of the few remaining supply ships that supplied Allies with much-needed supplies during the last World War. The ship tour and museum recall the sacrifice of many who served in the merchant marine at great loss of life.

3- Sparkman Wharf, a cultural extravaganza of food offerings and tastings of most every cuisine. The outdoor dining from rehabilitated shipping containers provides a short walking distance to its many waterfront dining options.

4- Tampa Riverwalk, the three-mile walk from the Tampa Bay History Center to Armature Works is a pedestrian pathway along the Hillsborough River complete with activities, sights, restaurants, shopping, and a monument trail featuring the area's history. Or take the trip by Pirate Water Taxi, with frequent stops along the way.

5- Tampa Bay History Center, a world-class museum featuring the history of the area from the Indigenous people of 10,000 years ago to the heyday of the cigar industry, to the Spanish-American War, pirate lore, and art exhibits of Florida's many species. The Columbia Restaurant café completes the experience.

6- Pirate Water Taxi has multiple stops along the Hillsborough River following the course of the Riverwalk.

7- Henry B. Plant Museum, located in what was Henry B. Plant's luxury Tampa Bay Hotel, now within the University of Tampa campus, portrays the elegance of the Gilded Age and the contributions made by Plant to the development of Florida. A great seasonal experience at Christmas.

8- Glazer Children's Museum is a unique museum with interactive exhibits that allow children to play while they learn.

9- Tampa Museum of Art covers the waterfront with its exhibits ranging from the ancient world to modern art and periods of art history in between. Its collections include sculpture, photography, and paintings. The museum provides art classes for all ages.

10- The Straz Center for the Performing Arts is one of the largest performing arts centers in the country with five theatres providing varying venues for plays, operas, jazz concerts, and other performing arts. If it's at the Straz, it's going to be an enjoyable event.

11. Armature Works is due west of Ybor City by way of Palm Avenue to a community of its own in Tampa Heights, where shopping, restaurants, and markets make up a community of people living, working, and enjoying life together. A great destination for date night.

Images in this "Just Beyond Ybor" section are provided courtesy of Visit Tampa Bay. Sparkman Wharf, the Henry B. Plant Museum, and Armature Works images, are courtesy of Keir Magoulas, Visit Tampa Bay. Aquarium scuba photo, courtesy of Lynn Nankervis, is of Matthew Nankervis in the foreground, used with permission.

In the next ten years, the redevelopment of the Channelside District, extending from Ybor City into Tampa, along the streetcar line will create new living space and more opportunities for business, shopping, and cultural growth, revitalizing this section of the city adjoining the Historic District.

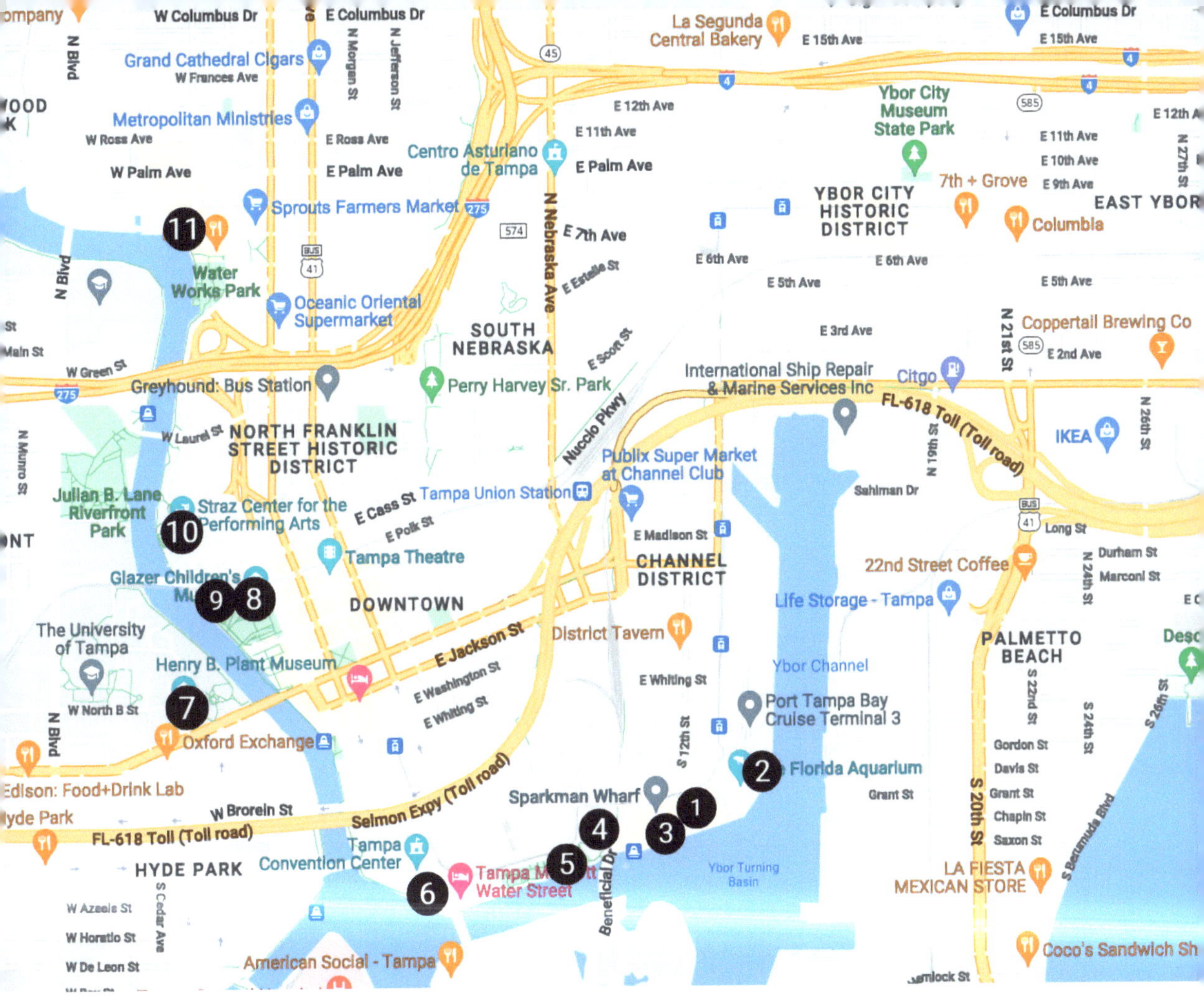

Ybor City archway lights installed along 7th Avenue, 2023.

Notes and Further Reading Suggestions

1. L. Glenn Westfall, *Don Vicente Martinez Ybor, the Man and His Empire* (New York: Garland Publishing, Inc., 1987), 40-46.

2. Westfall, *Don Vicente Martinez Ybor*, 44-45.

3. Frank T. Lastra, *Ybor City, The Making of a Landmark Town* (Tampa: University of Tampa Press, 2006), 12-13.

4. Wallace Reyes, *Once Upon a Time in Tampa . . . Rise and fall of the cigar industry . . .* (Scotts Valley, CA: CreateSpace Independent Publishing Platform, 2013), 53-55.

5. Reyes, *Once Upon a Time in Tampa*, 53-55; Westfall, *Don Vicente Martinez Ybor*, 68-69, 81-86.

6. Westfall, *Don Vicente Martinez Ybor*, 70-75, 155-158.

7. "About Us," Ybor City Museum Society, accessed June 2023, https://www.ybormuseum.org; "Ybor City Museum State Park," Florida State Parks, accessed June 2023, https://www.floridastate-parks.org/parks-and-trails/ybor-city-museum-state-park.

8. "Explore El Reloj," J.C. Newman Cigar Company, accessed June 2023, https://www.jcnewman.com/el-reloj/museumtheaterfactorystore/; Wallace Reyes, *Cigar City Architecture and Legacy* (Scotts Valley, CA: CreateSpace Independent Publishing Platform, 2015), 135-139.

9. "Welcome to the Tampa Baseball Museum," Tampa Baseball Museum at the Al Lopez House, accessed June 2023, https://www.tampabaseballmuseum.org/.

10. "Welcome to the Ybor City Visitor Information Center!" Ybor City Visitor Information Center, Ybor City Chamber of Commerce, accessed June 2023, https://www.ybor.org/vic/.

11. "About Us - Welcome," Centro Español de Tampa, accessed June 2023, http://centroespanoltampa.org/#AboutUS.

12. "History of El Circulo Cubano (Cuban Club)," The Cuban Club, accessed June 2023, http://cubanclubybor.com/history/.

13. "History," Centro Asturiano de Tampa, Centro Asturiano de Tampa, Inc., accessed June 2023, https://www.centroasturianotampa.org/history/.

14. Catherine Cueto, Kortlyn Dougherty, and Melina Santos, "Afro-Cubans in Ybor City, 1880s-Present, Part One," USF Department of Anthropology Digital Exhibits, https://usflibexhibits.omeka.net/exhibits/show/civil-rights-in-tampa/afro-cubans-1, accessed September 3, 2023

15. Judge E. J. Salcines, "History," The Italian Club, L'Unione Italiana, accessed June 2023, https://italian-club.org/history/.

16. "German-American Club of Tampa," Wikipedia, last modified August 29, 2022, accessed June 2023, https://en.wikipedia.org/wiki/German-American_Club_of_Tampa.

17. Reyes, email message to author in response to question of how many casitas were built in Ybor City, April 1, 2023.

18. Reyes, *Once Upon a Time in Tampa*, 66; Westfall, *Don Vicente Martinez Ybor*, 73-74.

19. Lastra, *Ybor City, The Making of a Landmark Town*, 29; "Henry B. Plant Biography," Henry B. Plant Museum, accessed June 2023, https://plantmuseum.com/about/henry-b-plant-bio.

20. Rodney Kite-Powell, "Tampa's Historic Streetcars," August 15,, 2023, Tampa Bay History Center, https://tampabayhistorycenter.org/blog/tampas-historic-streetcars/; Reyes, *Once Upon a Time in Tampa*, 48-49.

21. "Don Quixote Dining Room," Columbia Restaurant, Ybor City location, accessed June 2023, https://www.columbiarestaurant.com/don-quixote-dining-room.

22. "El Patio Dining Room," Columbia Restaurant, Ybor City location, accessed June 2023, https://www.columbiarestaurant.com/el-patio-dining-room.

23. Alfred J. López, *Josè Martí, A Revolutionary Life* (Austin: University of Texas Press, 2014), 265-266, 283-296.

24. John M. Dunn, *Josè Martí: Cuba's Greatest Hero* (Sarasota, FL: Pineapple Press, Inc., 2015), 81-90.

25. Reyes, *Once Upon a Time in Tampa*, 161-164, 171-182.

26. "Tampa Bay Historic Walking Tours," Tampa Bay Tours, accessed June 2023, https://tampa-bay-tours.com/.

27. "Our Tours," Ybor City Food Tours, accessed June 2023, https://yborcityfoodtours.com/tours/.

28. "Tampa's #1 Crime Tour/About Our Tampa Mafia Tours," Tampa Mafia, accessed June 2023, https://tampamafia.com/.

29. "Visit El Reloj, the Last-Operating Cigar Factory in Tampa, Fla.," J.C. Newman Cigar Company, accessed June 2023, https://www.jcnewman.com/visit-us/; Wallace Reyes, *Cigar City Architecture and Legacy* (Scotts Valley, CA: CreateSpace Independent Publishing Platform, 2015), 135-139.

30. "Florida Brewing Company, Florida's First Brewery," Harley Sharpton and the Tampa Historical Team, Tampa Historical, accessed June 2023, https://www.tampahistorical.org/items/show/134.

31. "Florida Brewing Company building, History," Wikipedia, accessed June 4, 2023, https://en.wikipedia.org/wiki/Florida_Brewing_Company_building; "Our History," Swope Rodante, accessed June 2023, https://www.swoperodante.com/our-firm/our-history/.

32. "Top Sellers," Columbia Restaurant Gift Shop, accessed June 2023, https://shop.columbiarestaurant.com/collections/top-sellers.

33. "About," Kress Contemporary, accessed September 2, 2023, https://www.kresscontemporary.com/about

34. "Memory Makers–Maria Esparza" Visit Tampa Bay, Interview, accessed June 2023, https://www.visittampabay.com/blog/archive/post/memory-maker-maria-esparza/.

35. Chico Garcia, *Viva Ybor*, 2012, mural, south side of 7th Avenue between 19th and 20th Streets.

36. Chico Garcia, *Viva Ybor*, 2023.

37. Cesar Gonzmart installed tile on the exterior of the Columbia Restaurant in the 1930s restoration by artist Judith Villavisanis. "The Story of the Tiles at the Columbia Restaurant in Tampa," Visit Florida, accessed June 2023, https://www.visitflorida.com/travel-ideas/articles/eat-drink-columbia-restaurant-tampa-tiles-tell-a-story-of-family-and-country/.

38. Content regarding The *Tampa Town* mural provided by artist and historian Joe King Carter, June 2021.

39. Paul Guzzo, "Tampa Mural Honors 5,000 Women Who Protested Fascism in 1937," Tampa Bay Times, updated April 5, 2023, https://www.tampabay.com/life-culture/history/2023/03/31/fascismybor-citywomwomens-history-monthspanish-civil-wardolores-ibrrurifrancisco-franco/.

40. "Historical Markers of Hillsborough: The 1937 Antifascist Women's March," Hillsborough County, posted April 26, 2023, accessed June 2023, https://www.hillsboroughcounty.org/en/newsroom/2023/04/26/historical-markers-of-hillsborough-the-1937-antifascist-womens-march#.

41. Martí-Maceo mural 2013, Historic Ybor City, Sociedad La Union Martí-Maceo building, contributor RKG/picfair.com, used under license.

42. James W. Covington, "The Rough Riders in Tampa," *Sunland Tribune*, vol. 3, article 2 (1977), available at Digital Commons @ University of South Florida, accessed June 2023,

https://digitalcommons.usf.edu/cgi/viewcontent.cgi?article=1018&context=sunlandtribune; Plaque adjacent to *The Charge of the Yellow Rice Brigade* mural, Roosevelt Reading Room and Library, Hotel Haya.

43. *An American Journey*, Ybor Art Project, accessed June 2023, https://yborartproject.com/.

44. Jay Giroux and Edgar Sanchez Cumbas, *Living Shades*, 2021, mural, east side of the Hillsborough Community College, Ybor Campus, https://www.hccfl.edu/campus-life/arts/hcc-art-galleries/grounds4art/past-grounds4art-projects, accessed August 2023.

45. Trinity Rivard, *Generations*, 2023, mural, between the Ybor Building and Faculty Building of the Hillsborough Community College, Ybor Campus, accessed August 2023, https://www.hccfledu/campus-life/arts/arts/galeries-hcc/grounds4art.

46. "Shophouse," Wikipedia, accessed June 2023, https://en.wikipedia.org/wiki/Shophouse.

47. Reyes, *Cigar City Architecture and Legacy*, 353-354.

48. Reyes, *Cigar City Architecture and Legacy*, (Coppell, TX: CreateSpace Independent Publishing, 2015), 345-347.

49. Reyes, *Cigar City Architecture and Legacy*, 337-340.

50. Reyes, *Cigar City Architecture and Legacy*, 325-326.

51. Reyes, *Cigar City Architecture and Legacy*, 327-328.

52. Reyes, *Cigar City Architecture and Legacy*, 349-352.

53. "Ybor City Arch-Tampa, FL-Freestanding Arches," Waymarking.com, https://www.waymarking.com/waymarks/WM6ZTQ.

54. Reyes, "Ybor City Lamp Post History," Facebook: Cuban Club 101, posted February 22, 2019, accessed 6/30/2023.

A piece of history in the not too distant past memorialized in Ybor City. Sculpture ***Fearless Champions*** by Becky Ault to honor the First Responders and those who they helped survive the fateful day of 911 in 2001. Use of stainless steel with a beam recovered from the wreckage. According to the State Department at least 102 countries lost citizens. Many killed had recently become U.S. citizens and included documented and undocumented immigrants. Their deaths reflect a world that is truly global, a diversity not defined by political boundaries.

Picture Index

PAGE NO.	DESCRIPTION	ATTRIBUTION	SPANISH	ITALIAN
	Descriptions of pictures are listed by page number and are described from those at the top of the page to the bottom and from left to right		Las descripciones de las imágenes se figuran por los números de las páginas y están descritos desde la parte superior de la página hasta la parte inferior y desde la izquierda hasta la derecha	Le descrizioni delle immagini sono elencate dal numero della pagina e sono descritte nella parte superiore in basso dalla sinistra alla destra.
Title Page	The Flor de Ybor City cigar label bears the name of the historic district	"The Flor de Ybor City (Ybor City Cigar Co.) logo and trademark is owned, and officially licensed by, Fuente Marketing Ltd."	La etiqueta de cigarro de la Flor de la Ciudad de Ybor lleva el nombre del distrito histórico	L' etichetta del sigaro Flor di Ybor City porta il nome del quartiere storico.
	"Y" medallion, center of Ybor City's archway lights on 7th Avenue	Photo by Phil Sauerbrun (PS)	El medallón "Y", centro de las luces del arco de la Ciudad de Ybor, en la 7a Avenida	Medaglione "Y" centro delle luci dell'arco della città nella via settima.
TOC2	Palm tree lined La Setima, designated One of America's Ten Great Streets	Courtesy of Keir Magoulas, Visit Tampa Bay	La Sétima, bordeada de palmeras, designada como una de las diez gran calles de América.	La Setima fiancheggiata da palme, designata come una delle dieci grandi strade d'America
1	Centro Ybor District established in 2000 to be a multipurpose business, dining, and entertainment center	Courtesy of Keir Magoulas, Visit Tampa Bay	El Distrito del Centro Ybor fue establecido en el año 2000 para ser un centro de múltiples negocios de restaurantes y entretenimiento	Quartiere del Centro Ybor fondato nel anno 2000 some un centro dei affari, ristorante e l'intrattenimento
3	Photo of Don Vicente Martínez-Ybor, circa 1890	Vicente Martínez-Ybor, circa 1890, unknown author, source: Tampa Bay History Center, P.D.-US.	Foto de Don Vicente Martínez-Ybor, hacia 1890	Foto di Don Vicente Martínez-Ybor, circa 1890.
3	Bronze statue of Ybor in Centro Ybor	Courtesy of Dave Decker Photography	Estatua de bronce de Ybor en el Centro Ybor	Statua in bronzo di Ybor nel Centro Ybor.
5	Casitas (little houses) for cigar workers	Courtesy of Keir Magoulas Photography	Las Casitas para los fabricantes de cigarros	Le casette per i lavoratori del sigaro.
6	Ybor Cigar Factory, N. 14th Street at E. 9th Avenue	Photo by PS	La Fábrica de Cigarros de Ybor, Calle 14 Norte en la Avenida 9 Este	La fabbrica Ybor City, strada 14 nord nella strada 9 est.
7	Ybor City Museum State Park	Photo by PS	El Museo de la Ciudad de Ybor	Il Parco Statale del museo della città di Ybor.

8	Museum exhibits tell the story of Ybor City	Photo by PS. Ybor Cigar Factory image, Historical Collection Tampa-Hillsborough County Public Library. Wikipedia, History of Ybor City, CC BY-SA, P.D.-US.	Las exhibiciones del muses describen la historia del la Ciudad de Ybor	Le mostra del museo raccontano la storia della citta' di Ybor
9	The Ybor Seal created by historian Anthony ("Tony") P. Pizzo	Courtesy of Arminda Mata, President and CEO, Ybor City Museum Society.	El Sello de Ybor creado por el historiador, Anthony ("Tony") P. Pizzo	IL Sigillo Ybor creato dallo storico Anthony (Tony) Pizzo.
9	Museum Garden adjacent to the museum	Photo by PS.	El Jardín Estatal del Museo adyacente al museo	Il Giardino del Museo accanto al museo.
10	Bust of Vicente Martínez-Ybor in the Museum Garden	Photo by PS	El Busto de Vicente Martínez-Ybor en el Jardín del Museo	Il Busto di Vicente Martínez-Ybor nel Giardino del Museo.
10	Interior rooms of a casita on the Ybor City Museum State Park's Casita Tour.	Courtesy of Ashley Smith. "10 ways to Spend a Day in Ybor City, Tampa" | My Wanderlusty Life. Https://www.mywanderlustylife.com/one-day-in-ybor-city-tampa/. Travel blog by Ashley Smith	Los cuartos interiores de una Casita en el Tour de Casita del Parque Estatal del Museo de la Ciudad de Ybor	Le stanze interne di una casetta durante un giro del Parco Statale del Museo della Città di Ybor.
11	J.C. Newman Factory, El Reloj	Photo by PS	La Fábrica J.C. Newman, El Reloj	J.C. Newman Factory, L'Orologio.
12	J.C. Newman Cigar Co. foyer, museum, and rolling floor	Courtesy of J.C. Newman Cigar Co.	J.C. Newman Cigar Co. vestíbulo, museo y piso de liar cigarros	J.C. Newman Cigar Co.,l'ingresso, il museo e la stanza per il lavoro dei sigari
13	Tampa Baseball Museum at the Al Lopez House, main museum floor, and Lou Piniella display.	Exterior photo courtesy of Chantal Hevia. Courtesy of Arminda Mata, President and CEO, Ybor City Museum Society	El Museo de Béisbol de Tampa en la Casa Al López, piso principal del museo y la exhibición de Lou Piniella	Tampa Baseball Museum nella casa di Al Lopez, la stanza principale e la mostra di Lou Pinella
14	Ybor City Chamber Visitor Information Center in Centro Ybor on E. 8th Avenue	Photo by PS	El Centro de Información para Visitantes de la Cámara de la Ciudad de Ybor en Centro Ybor, en la Avenida 8 Este	Centro Informazioni Turistiche della città di Ybor nel centro di Ybor nella Via 8 est.
15	Visitor Information Center theatre room and map of historic sites.	Photo by PS	Centro de Información para Visitantes, Sala de Teatro y mapa de lugares históricos	Centro informazione Turistiche sala del teatro e la piantina dei siti storici
16	Statue of Queen Isabella, carved wood, commissioned by Vicente Martínez-Ybor	Courtesy of PamElla Lee Photography	La Estatua de la Reina Isabela, madera tallada, encargada por Vicente Martínez-Ybor	La statua della Regina Isabella, legno intagliato, commissionata da Vicente Martínez-Ybor

18	Spanish Community Center (El Centro Español de Tampa)	El Centro Español de Tampa, Tampa AGS Media, Creative Commons, Attribution-Share Alike 3.0 Unported license (CC BY-SA 3.0) https://creativecommons.org/licenses/by-sa/3.0/deed.en	El Centro Español de Tampa	Il Centro Comunitario Spagnolo (El Centro Espanol de Tampa).
18	The Birth of Mutual Aid Societies in America Historical Marker	Photo by PS	El Nacimiento de las Sociedades de Ayuda Mutua en el Marcador Histórico de América	La nascita delle società del mutuo soccorso, nel cartello storico d'America.
19	The Cuban Club (El Circulo Cubano) front view, N. 14th Street, bust of José Martí on the right	Photo by PS	La vista frontal del Club Cubano (El Círculo Cubano), Calle 14 Norte, busto de José Martí a la derecha	Il Club Cubano (El Circulo Cubano) vista frontale, Via 14 nord, busto di José Martí' a destra.
19	Stained Glass Window of the Cuban Coat of Arms	Photo by PS	La Ventana Vitral del Escudo de Armas Cubano	La finestra istoriata della Stemma Cubana.
20	Group tour from *Buildings Alive* led by Cristal Lastra, President of the Centro Asturiano Board of Directors; Centro Asturiano's refurbished theatre; and exterior at night.	Courtesy of Arminda Mata, President and CEO, Ybor City Museum Society	Grupo de una excursión de Buildings Alive liderado por Cristal Lastra, Presidenta de la Junta Directiva del Centro Asturiano, el reformado teatro del Centro Asturiano y su exterior de noche	Un gruppo di partecipante di Buildings Alive, con la guida Cristal Lastra, Presidente del Consiglio di Amministrazione del Centro Asturiano
21	El Centro Asturiano de Tampa, Nebraska Avenue	Photo by PS	El Centro Asturiano de Tampa, Avenida Nebraska	Il Club Asturiano (El Centro Asturiano de Tampa), Via Nebraska nord.
22	The Martí-Maceo Society (Sociedad La Union Martí-Maceo)	Photo by PS	La Sociedad Martí-Maceo (La Sociedad La Unión Martí-Maceo)	La Società Martí-Maceo (Sociedad La Union Martí-Maceo).
22	Painted tile sign of Martí and Maceo near front door of the Martí-Maceo Society	Photo by PS	El cartel del azulejo pintado de Martí y Maceo cerca de la puerta frontal de la Sociedad Martí-Maceo	Il cartello a piastrelle di Martí e Maceo vicino l'entrata della Martí-Maceo Society.
23	The Italian Club (L'Unione Italiana) at night	Courtesy of Scott M. Deitche	El Club Italiano (L'Unione Italiana) de noche	L'Unione Italiana di notte.

24	The cultural clubs have facilities rentable for special events. Second floor Lobby of the Italian Center at Christmas, the Connie Spoto Walter Theatre, and the Capitano Grand Ballroom	Photos courtesy of the Italian Club, Mark Stanish	Vestíbulo del segundo piso del Centro Italiano en Navidad, el Teatro Connie Spoto Walker y el Gran Salón de Baile Capitano	Atrio al secondo piano dell'Unione Italiana durante Natale,. Il Teatro Walter Connie Spoto e la sala di ballo Capitano.
25	German-American Club (Deutsch Amerikanischer Verein) building fronting Nebraska Avenue	Photo by PS	El edificio del Club Alemán-Americano (Deutsh Amerikanischer Verein) frente a la Avenida Nebraska	L'Edificio del Club Tedesco-Americano (Deutsh Amerikanischer Verein) davanti a Via Nebraska.
26	South side of German-American Club	Photo by PS	El lado sur del Club Alemán-Americano	Lato sud del Club Tedesco-Americano.
27	Casitas on 9th Avenue next to the Ybor City Museum State Park	Photo by PS	Casitas en la 9a Avenida, al lado del Parque Estatal del Museo de la Ciudad de Ybor	Casette nella via 9 vicino al parco statale del museo della città di Ybor.
29	Streetcars initially pulled by a woodburning steam engine on a narrow gauge track in the late 1880s	Crew and train of Tampa Street Railway-Tampa, Florida. 1886-04. State Archives of Florida, Florida Memory. Common Domain, https://www.floridamemory.com/items/show/26055	Los tranvías inicialmente jalados por una máquina de vapor de leña en una vía estrecha al final de la década de 1880	Tram inizialmente tirati da un motore vapore a legno sul binario stretto.
30	Maintenance facility for the TECO streetcar line, located in Ybor City	TECO line cars in the maintenance yard. From Railfann99. Creative Commons Attribution-Share Alike 4.0 International License, https://commons Wikimedia.org/wiki/File: Tecolinecars.jpg	El centro de mantenimiento para la línea de tranvía de TECO, ubicado en la Ciudad de Ybor	Il servizio di manutenzione per la linea del tram TECO, situata nella città di Ybor.
31	Vintage wood interior of the streetcar	Interior of a TECO car. 2020. Peter K. Burian. Creative Commons Attribution-Share Alike 4.0, CC BY-SA 4.0. https://www.wikiwand.com/en/Centro_Ybor_Station#Media/File:Interior_of_a_historic_streetcar_Ybor_City,_Tampa,_Florida.jpg	La madera vintage del interior del tranvía	L'interno del tram fatto di legno vintage.

32	The streetcar route operates on a single track with passing sidings at frequent intervals.	Courtesy of Keir Magoulas, Visit Tampa Bay	La ruta del tranvía opera en una sola vía con apartaderos de paso a intervalos frecuentes.	Il percorso del tram funziona in un unico binario.
32	Tampa's Union Station, exterior, located at 601 N. Nebraska Avenue	Italian Renaissance Style Front façade of the 1912 Tampa Union Station. TampAGS, for AGS Media - Own work, CC BY-SA 3.0, https://commons.wikimedia.org/w/index.php?curid=8894769	La Estación Unión de Tampa, exterior, ubicada en la Avenida Nebraska, 601 Norte	L'esterno della Union Station di Tampa, situata in Via Nebraska, 601 nord.
33	Columbia Restaurant fronts E. 7th Avenue between N 21st and 22nd streets	Photo by PS	El Restaurante Columbia, está ubicado frente la Avenida 7 Este entre las Calles 21 y 22 Norte	Il ristorante Colombia, di fronte alla 7° Via tra la strada 21 e 22 nord.
34	Tile mural depicting a scene from Don Quixote, a novel by Miguel de Cervantes, exterior Columbia Restaurant	Photo by PS	El mural de azulejo representando una escena de Don Quijote, una novela de Miguel de Cervantes, exterior del Restaurante Columbia	Murale di piastrelle che mostra una scena di Don Chisciotte, un romanzo di Miquel Cervantes, all'esterno del ristorante Colombia.
35	El Patio Dining Room, the Columbia Restaurant	Courtesy of the Columbia Restaurant	El Patio Comedor, el Restaurante Columbia	La sala da pranzo El Patio, del ristorante Colombia.
36	Exterior tiled walls of the Columbia Restaurant at one of the entrances	Photo by PS	Las paredes exteriores de azulejos del Restaurante Columbia en una de las entradas	Pareti esterne di piastrelle all'entrata del ristorante Colombia.
36	The Columbia Restaurant's lighted corner on 7th Avenue at night	Photo by PS	La esquina iluminada por el Restaurante Columbia en la 7ª Avenida, de noche	L'angolo illuminato del Colombia Restaurant nella via 7 di notte
37	José Martí, c. 1893	Photo of José Martí (1853-1895) taken by 1895. Unknown Source, Unknown author, Public Domain, U.S. via Wikimedia Commons/ https://commons.wikimedia.org/wiki/File:José-Martí.jpg	José Martí, 1893	José Martí, 1893.
37	Statue of José Martí in the Friends of José Martí Park	Courtesy of Dave Decker Photography	La estatua de José Martí en el Parque Conmemorativo de José Martí	La statua di José Martí nel Parco Memoriale di José Martí.

38	1893 photo of José Martí on the steps of Vicente Martínez-Ybor factory with cigar workers	José Martí on the iron steps of a cigar factory where he made a speech for Cuban Independence 1890 (circa). State Archives of Florida, Florida Memory Collections, P.D., https://www.floridamemory.com/items/sho/30571	Foto de 1893 de José Martí en los escalones de la Fábrica de Vicente Martínez-Ybor con los fabricantes de cigarros	Foto del 1893 di José Martí' sulle scale della fabbrica Vicente Martínez-Ybor con i lavoratori dei sigari.
39	Enter into The Friends of José Martí Park and you're on Cuban soil	Courtesy of Keir Magoulas, Visit Tampa Bay	Entre en el Parque de Los Amigos de José Martí y está en suelo cubano	L'angolo illuminato del Colombia Restaurant nella via 7 di notte
40	Lt. Colonel Theodore Roosevelt and the Rough Riders at San Juan Hill in Cuba, 1898	Rough Riders at the Batttle of San Juan Hill in Santiago de Cuba in July 1898. William Dinwiddle. Library of Congress Prints and Photographs Division. Digital ID cph.3a10269. US Public Domain extracted from Rough Riders, Wikimedial Commons.	El Teniente Coronel Theodore Roosevelt y los Jinetas Rudos (Rough Riders) en el Cierro de San Juan en Cuba, 1898	Il tenente colonnello Theodore Roosevelt e I Rough Riders nella collina di San Juan Cuba, 1898.
40	Memorial Plaque in Rough Riders Park at E. 7th Avenue and Nuccio Parkway	Photo by PS	Placa conmemorativa en el Parque Jinetas Rudos (Rough Riders Park) en las Avenidas 7 Este y Nuccio	La targa commemorativa nel parco Rough Riders nella Via 7° est e Nuccio Parkway.
41	Entrance to Tabanero Cigars, on E. 7th Avenue	Photo by PS	La Entrada a Cigarros Tabanero, en la Avenida 7 Este	L'ingresso ai sigari Tabanero, nella Via 7°.
42	Female cigar roller at La Faraona Cigar Shop E. 7th Avenue	Photo by PS	Mujer fabricante de cigarros en la Tabaquería Faraona, Avenida 7 Este	Una lavoratrice del sigaro nella Faraona Cigar Shop, nella Via 7°.
43	Hand-rolling a cigar at J.C. Newman Co. Cigar Factory	Courtesy of J.C. Newman Cigar Co.	Liando un cigarro a mano en La Fábrica de la Compañía de Cigarro J.C.Newman	Come fare un sigaro a mano alla Fabbrica J.C. Newman.
43	Mechanized equipment used in cigar manufacture at J.C. Newman Cigar Co.	Courtesy of J.C. Newman Cigar Co.	Equipo mecanizado usado en la fabricación de cigarros en J.C. Newman Cigar Co.	Apparecchiatura utilizzata per la produzione dei sigari nella Fabbrica J.C. Newman cigar Co.
44	Modern humidor with individual lockers at Tabanero Cigars	Photo by PS.	Humidor (de cigarros) moderno con armarios individuales en Cigarros Tabanero	Humidor moderno con armadietti individuali a Tabanero Cigars aziendale.

44	International headquarters of Arturo Fuente on N 22nd Street and E 2nd Avenue. Logo of Arturo Fuente on its warehouse renovated in 2016 adjacent to its original factory also renovated for its corporate offices	Photo by PS	El Cuartel International de Arturo Fuentes en la Calle 22 N. y la 2ª Avenida E. El logo de Arturo Fuente en el almacén restaurado en 2016 adyacente a su fábrica original también restaurada para sus oficinas corporativas	Sede internazionale di Arturo Fuente alla strada 22 e via 2 Logo di Arturo Fuente sul suo magazzino ristrutturato nel 2016.
45	Holden Rasmussen, historian for J.C. Newman Cigar Co., begins his tour in the company museum	Courtesy of J.C. Newman Cigar Co.	Holden Rasmussen, historiador de la Compañía de Cigarros JC Newman, comienza su tour en el museo de la compañía	Holden Rasmussen, storico di J.C. Newman Cigar Company inizia un giro nel museo aziendale.
46	Clock tower of the J. C. Newman Cigar Co. Factory	Photo by PS	La Torre del Reloj de la Fábrica de la Compañía de Cigarros J.C.Newman	La torre dell'orologio della fabbrica di sigari J.C. Newman Company.
47	Max Herman gestures to El Pasaje, originally Vicente Martínez-Ybor's office building, on an evening ghost tour	Photo courtesy of Tampa Bay Tours, Ybor City Historic Walking Tours	Max Hermán hace gesto a El Pasaje, originalmente el edificio de oficinas de Vicente Martínez-Ybor, en un recorrido nocturno de fantasmas	Max Herman indica El Pasaje, originariamente l'edificio degli uffici per Vicente Martínez-Ybor, in un giro serale dei fantasmi.
48	Cindi Hughlett from the Ybor City Food Tour, introducing the Visitor Information Center's video to a tour group	Photo by PS. Used with permission.	Cindi Hughlett del Recorrido de Comida de la Ciudad de Ybor, presentándole a un grupo de turistas un video del Centro de Información	Hughlett dell'Ybor Food Tour, presentando il video a un gruppo di turisti nel Centro Informazione Turistica.
49	Scott M. Deitche, author and tour leader for Tampa Mafia Tours, superimposed on his bestselling "Cigar City Mafia" book	Courtesy of Scott M. Deitche	Scott M. Deitche, autor y líder los Recorridos de la Mafia de Tampa, superpuso en su libro superventas, "Cigar City Mafia" ("Mafia de la Ciudad de Cigarros")	Scott M. Deitche, autore e guida di Tampa Mafia Tours, sovrapposto al suo libro bestseller, Cigar City Mafia.
50	Florida Brewing Co. building as it appears today renovated for the Swope, Rodante law firm who occupy the building	Photo by PS	El edificio de la Compañía de Cervecera de la Florida como aparece hoy renovado para el bufete de Abogados Swope, Rodante quien ocupa el edificio	Florida Brewing Company edificio com'è oggi ristrutturato per lo studio legale Swope, Rodante che occupa l'edificio.

52	Florida Brewing Co. building as it appeared in 1898 at 5th Avenue near N. 13th Street	The Florida Brewing Company and the Ybor Ice Works, 1894. Tony Pizzo Collection, Creator: Burgert Brothers, Date: 1897. USF Tampa Library, Special and Digital Collections, https://tampahistorical.org/items/show/134	El edificio de la Compañía de Cervecera de la Florida (Florida Brewing Co.) tal como apareció en 1898 en la 5a Avenida cerca de la Calle 13 Norte	L'edificio della Florida Brewing Company come sembrava nel 1898 in Via 5° vicino alla strada 13°.
53	Artist Terry Klaaren's mural depicting the Florida Brewing Co. and its surrounding support buildings at the time of their construction	Photo courtesy of Swope Rodante, Darrien Bagley, photographer	El mural del artista Terry Klaaren mostrando La Compañía de Cervecera de la Florida y sus edificios de apoyo que rodean en el tiempo de su construcción	Il murale dell'artista Terry Klaren che mostra la Florida Brewing Company e i suoi edifici di sostegno al momento della loro costruzione.
53	Widescreen photo of the Florida Brewery Company building, now Swope, Rodante Law Firm.	Photo courtesy of Swope Rodante, Darrien Bagley, photographer	Foto panorámica del edificio de la vieja Compañía de Cervecera de la Florida, ahora el bufete de Abogados Swope, Rodante	Foto panoramica del vecchio edificio della Florida Brewing Company, adesso studio legale Swope, Rodante
54	Historical marker identifying the significance of the location of the brewery	Photo by PS	Marcador histórico identificando el significado de la localización de la cervecería	Il cartello storico che identifica l'importanza del sito del birrificio.
55	The Brick's Café entrance on 7th Avenue at 14th Street	Photo by PS	La entrada del Café Bricks en la 7ª Avenida, en la Calle 14	L'entrata di Bricks Café' alla via 7 e la strada 14
56	Monthly luncheon of the Ybor City Chamber of Commerice in the Siboney Dining Room of the Columbia Restaurant.	Courtesy of PamElla Lee Photography	Almuerzo mensual de la Cámara de Comercio de la Ciudad de Ybor en el Comedor Siboney del Restaurante Columbia	Il pranzo mensile della Camera di Commercio della città di Ybor nella sala da pranzo nel ristorante Columbia.
56	Two popular restaurants on 7th Avenue, Roast and 7th + Grove	Photo by PS	Dos restaurantes populares en la 7 a Avenida, Roast y 7 a + Grove	Due ristoranti popolari nella 7° via, Roast e 7th + Grove.
57	Pizza thrown in Due Amici's front window on 7th Avenue, the front entrance to Carmine's and sign for Devil Crab.	Photo by PS	Pizza tirada en la ventana delantera de Due Amici, en la 7ª Avenida, la entrada principal de Carmine's y el letrero de Devil Crab	La pizza fatto a mano alla ventrina del ristorante Due Amici alla via 7: l'entrata del ristorante Carmine's ed il cartello per Devil Crabs
59	Ybor City's historic bakery, La Segunda, at 2512 N. 15th Street at 15th Avenue	Photo by PS	La Pastelería histórica de la Ciudad de Ybor, La Segunda, Calle 15, 2512 Norte	La panetteria storica della citta' di Ybor, La Segunda, nella strada 15a, 2512 nord.

60	The line frequently to the door of La Segunda but the wait is worth it.	Photo by PS	La frecuente cola hasta la puerta de La Segunda, pero la espera vale la pena	Spesso c'e' una fila alla porta di La Segunda, ma vale la pena di aspettare
60	A street sign promotes four of Ybor City's comfort foods.	Courtesy of PamElla Photography	Un letrero en la calle promociona cuatro de las comidas más reconfortantes de la Ciudad de Ybor	Un cartello per quattro cibi popolari di Ybor City
61	Front window of Agora, an "old world store," featuring products from all over the world	Courtesy of Agora	La ventana frontal de Agora, una "tienda del viejo mundo", con productos de alrededor del mundo	La vetrina di Agora, un "negozio del vecchio mondo", con i prodotti provenienti da tutto il mondo.
62	Image of the interior of Agora and the many colors of its products	Courtesy of Agora	Imagen del interior de Agora y los muchos colores de sus productos	Immagine interiore di Agora e dei suoi prodotti dai molteplici colori.
63	Front window of La France, a vintage clothing store for men and women	Courtesy of La France	Ventana frontal de La Francia (La France), una tienda de ropa antigua para hombres y mujeres	La vetrina di La France, un negozio di abbigliamento vintage per uomini e donne.
63	Jill Wax and son Ben behind the counter of their vintage clothing store, La France	Photo by PS, used with permission	Jill Wax e hijo Ben detrás del mostrador de su tienda de ropa antigua, La Francia (La France)	Jill Wax e suo figlio Ben dietro il balcone del suo negozio di abbigliamento vintage, La France.
63	Interior of La France	Courtesy of La France	Interior de La Francia (La France)	Interno di La France.
64	Décor setting at Dysfunctional Grace Art Company	Courtesy of Dysfunctional Grace	Decoración en la Compañía de Arte Dysfunctional Grace	Scena alla Dysfunctional Grace Art Company
65	Gift shop area of the Ybor City Chamber Visitor Information Center	Photo by PS, used with permission	Área de la tienda de regalos de la Cámara de la Ciudad de Ybor del Centro de Información para Visitantes	L'area del negozio di souvenir del Centro Informazione Turistica.
66	Display devoted to the art of Ferdie Pacheco	Photo by PS	Una muestra dedicada al arte de Ferdie Pacheco	Mostra dedicata all'arte di Ferdie Pacheco.
66	Two T-shirt offerings	Photo by PamElla Lee Photography, used with permission	Dos ofertas de camisetas	Due camicette in offerta.
67	Corner entrance to the Columbia Restaurant Gift Shop featuring the restaurant's cooking and food products as well as Spanish pottery	Photo by PS	Entrada de esquina a la Tienda de Regalos del Restaurante Columbia ofreciendo productos de cocina y alimenticias y también cerámica española	L'ingresso del ristorante Columbia Gift Shop con i prodotti culinari e alimentari del ristorante anche della ceramica spagnola.
67	7th Avenue entrance to the Columbia Restaurant Gift Shop	Photo by PS	Entrada de la 7a Avenida a la Tienda de Regalos del Restaurante Columbia	L'ingresso alla Colombia Gift Shop, via 7°.

68	View of the Saturday Market in Centennial Park from E. 9th Avenue	Photo by PS	Vista del Mercado de los sábados en el Parque Centenario (Centennial Park) desde la Avenida 9 Este	La vista del mercato del sabato nel Centennial Park di via 9°.
69	View of the Saturday Market from the streetcar line on E. 8th Avenue	Photo by PS	Vista del Mercado de los sábados desde la línea de tranvía en la Avenida 8 Este	La vista del mercato del sabato dalla linea del tram in via 8° est.
69	Vintage Roost warehouse view of furnishings	Courtesy of Vintage Roost	Vista de muebles del almacén Vintage Roost	Vista dell'arredamento del magazzino, Vintage Roost.
70	Furnishings featured at Stained Market Place	Courtesy of Stained Market Place	Muebles mostrados en El Sitio del Mercado Vitra (Stained Market Place)	L'arredamento del Stained Glass Market.
70	Stained Market Place logo	Courtesy of Stained Market Place	El logo de El Sitio del Mercado Vitra (Stained Market Place)	Il Logo-Stained Glass Market.
72	Kress Building houses the Kress Contemporary artists including the Florida Museum of Photographic Arts and the Tampa Ballet	Photo courtesy of Dave Decker Photography	El Edificio Kress aloja a los artistas del Contemporáneo Kress incluyendo al Museo de Artes Fotográficas de la Florida y el Ballet de Tampa	L'edificio Kress, che alloggia gli artisti contemporanei Kress con Florida Museum of Photographic Arts ed il Tampa Ballet.
73	Aerial view of the Kress Building	Photo courtesy of Dave Decker Photography	Vista aérea del Edificio Kress	La vista aerea dell'edificio, Kress.
74	Kress Contemporary artists and organizations	Graphic courtesy of Tracey Midulla	Los artistas del Contemporáneo Kress y organizaciones	Gli artisti contemporani e le organizzazioni.
76	Cinemagraphic art display from Tempus Volta, Ghost Orchid	Photo courtesy of Tempus Projects	La exhibición del arte cinematográfico de Tempus Volta, Orquídea de Fantasma (Ghost Orchid)	La mostra d'arte cinematografica di Tempus Volta, Orchidea fantasma (Ghost Orchid).
78	Members of the ballet group representing its diversity	Photo courtesy of Tampa City Ballet, Michael Sheehan photographer	Miembros del grupo de ballet representando su diversidad	I membri del gruppo del balletto che rappresentano la sua diversità'.
78	Scene from the Ballet's production, 7th Ave & Ybor	Photo courtesy of Tampa City Ballet, Soho Images (Haselwood, Herhige)	Escena de la producción del Ballet, 7a Avenida y Ybor	La scena della produzione del Balletto, Via 7° e Ybor.
79	Photos part of the collection of the Florida Museum of Photographic Arts	Courtesy of Florida Museum of Photographic Arts	Fotos parte de la colección del Museo de Artes Fotográficas de la Florida	Le fotografie della collezione del Florida Museum of Photographic Arts.
80	Images from Hillsborough Community College, Ybor Campus, Visual and Performing Arts	Courtesy of HCC, Ybor Campus Visual and Performing Arts	Imágenes de la Escuela Universitaria Comunitaria de Hillsborough (HCC), Campus de Ybor, Artes Visuales y Escénicas	Immagini di Hillsborough Community College, Ybor Campus, Arte Visuale e dello spettacolo Teatrale.

81	Storefront of Marcolina's Fine Arts Gallery	Photo courtesy of Marcolina's Fine Arts Gallery, Marcolina Mercado-Perez photographer	Escaparate de la Galería de Bellas Artes de Marcolina	La vetrina della Galleria delle Belle Arti di Marcolina.
82	Image of painting class at Marcolina's Fine Arts Gallery	Photo courtesy of Marcolina's Fine Arts Gallery, Marcolina Mercado-Perez photographer	imagen de una clase de pintura en la Galería de Bellas Artes de Marcolina	Immagine della lezione di pittura nella Galleria delle Belle Arti di Marcolina.
83	Two art books of Pacheco sold in the Ybor Visitor Center	Photo by PS	Dos libros de arte de Pacheco vendidos en el Centro de Visitantes de Ybor	Due libri d'arte di Pacheco venduti nel Centro Turistico di Ybor.
84	Paintings of Ybor street scenes by Joe King Carter	Courtesy of Joe King Carter	Pinturas de escenas callejeras de Ybor por Joe King Carter	I dipinti di scene stradale di Ybor, fatto da Joe King Carter.
84	Two portraits of historical figures drawn by Ron Watson, Paulina Pedroso on the left and Don Vicente Martínez-Ybor on the right	Courtesy of Ron Watson. Used with permission.	Dos retratos de figuras históricas por Ron Watson, Paulina Pedroso a la izquierda y Don Vicente Martínez-Ybor a la derecha	Due ritratti dei personaggi storici disegnati da Ron Watson: a sinistra, Paulina Pedroso e a destra il Don Vicente Martínez-Ybor.
85	Maria Esparza, artistic dance director for the Tampa Bay Flamenco Dance Company, strikes a pose in the troupe's dressing room prior to taking the stage	Courtesy of the Tampa Bay Flamenco Dance Company	María Esparza directora de danza artística para La Compañía de Baile Flamenco de la Bahía de Tampa, posa en el vestuario de la compañía antes de tomar el escenario	Maria Esparza, direttrice artistica della danza flamenco della Tampa Bay Flamenco Dance Company, in posa nel camerino della troupe, prima di entrare in teatro.
86	Flamenco Dance Company performs at the Columbia Restaurant on an evening dinner schedule six days a week	Photo courtesy of the Tampa Bay Flamenco Dance Company	La Compañía de Baile Flamenco realiza en el Restaurante Columbia en un horario de cena por la noche, seis días a la semana	La compagnia della danza del flamenco che da uno spettacolo al ristorante Columbia durante la cena, sei giorni alla settimana.
86	Formal picture of the dance group from the balcony of the El Patio Dining Room of the Columbia Restaurant	Photo courtesy of the Tampa Bay Flamenco Dance Company	Retrato formal del grupo de baile desde el balcón del Comedor El Patio del Restaurante Columbia	Foto formale del gruppo di danza dal balcone nella sala da pranzo El Patio del ristorante Colombia.
87	Artist Chico Garcia's first *Viva Ybor* mural depicting symbols and icons of Tampa and Ybor City	Image used under commercial license from Picfair.com	El primer mural Viva Ybor del artista Chico García representando símbolos e iconos de Tampa y la Ciudad de Ybor	Il primo murale dell'artista Chico Garcia mostra i simboli di Tampa e la Citta di Ybor.
88	Current mural similar to the first but also somewhat different	Photo by PS, Artist Chico Garcia, chicolesnyc.	Mural corriente similar al primero pero también en tanto diferente	Murale simile al primo ma anche un po'diverso.

89	Exterior tile mural at the Columbia Restaurant depicting the coming ashore by Columbus and his expedition in 1492	Photo by PS	Mural exterior de azulejos en el Restaurante Columbia representando la llegada a tierra de Colón y su expedición en 1492	Murale esterno al Ristorante Colombia che rappresenta l'arrivo a terra di Colombo e la sua spedizione nel 1492.
90 - 91	*Tampa Town* mural, created by Joe King Carter and Dave Audet, to represent the life and times of Ybor City, Tampa, its people and its culture. Inset photo of Carter and Audet during the mural's creation.	Image courtesy of Dave Decker Photography. Used with permission of Joe King Carter and Dave Audet. Inset, courtesy of Joe King Carter	Mural del Pueblo de Tampa, creado por Joe King Carter y Dave Audet, para representar la vida y los tiempos de la Ciudad de Ybor, Tampa, su gente y su cultura. Foto insertada de Carter y Audet durante la creación del mural	Il murale di Tampa Town, creato da Joe King Carter e David Audet, che rappresenta la vita ed i tempi della Citta di Ybor, Tampa, la sua gente e la sua cultura. Fotografia di Carter e Audet durante la creazione del murale
92	Mural represents the strong opposition of Ybor community women in a march organized and led by the women of Ybor City and Tampa against fascism in 1937	Photo by PS	Mural representa la fuerte oposición de las mujeres en la comunidad de Ybor en una marcha organizada y dirigida por las mujeres de la Ciudad de Ybor y Tampa contra el fascismo en 1937	Il murale rappresenta la forte opposizione delle donne della communita' di Ybor durante una marcia organizzata e guidata dalle donne della Citta di Ybor e di Tampa contro il fascismo del 1937.
93	Both sides of the historical marker give context to the nearby antifascism mural at 2015 E. 7th Avenue	Photo by PS	Ambos lados del marcador histórico dan contexto al mural cercano antifascista en la Avenida 7 Este, 2015	In entrambi i lati il cartello storico da contesto vicino al murale antifascista in Via 7° est, 2015.
94 - 95	Mural on the west side of the Sociedad La Union Martí-Maceo building is from a photo taken soon after its completion	Photo used under a commercial license with Picfair.com. City of Tampa mural collection. Artist: Derick Washington, Title: Wall of Martinez	Mural en el lado oeste del edificio de la Sociedad La Unión Martí-Maceo es de una foto tomada poco después de su terminación	Il murale sul lato ovest dell'edificio della Sociedad La Union Martí-Maceo. Foto fatta subito dopo il completamento.
96	In the Roosevelt Room at Hotel Haya resides an oil on canvas mural of Theodore Roosevelt entitled, The *Charge of the Yellow Rice Brigade*	Photo by PS	En la Sala Roosevelt en el Hotel Haya reside un mural de óleo sobre lienzo de Theodore Roosevelt titulado, La Carga de la Brigada del Arroz Amarillo	Nella Roosevelt Room nel Hotel Haya c'e' un murale d'olio di Theodore Roosevelt intitolato, The Charge of the Yellow Rice Brigade.
97	Google Earth image of the *American Journey* mural on Adamo Avenue	Google Earth image used to obtain an accurate rendering of the entire length of the mural	Imagen de Google Earth del mural del Viaje Americano (American Journey) en la Avenida Alamo	Immagine di Google Earth del murale American Journey in Via Adamo.
97	*Living Shades*, a mural on the campus of Hillsborough Community College, Ybor Campus	Courtesy of Hillsborough Community College, Ybor Campus, Department of Visual and Performaing Arts, by artists Jay Giroux and Edgar Sanchez Cumbas	Living Shades, un mural en el campus de la Escuela Universitaria Comunitaria de Hillsborough (HCC) Campus de Ybor	Living Shades, un murale nel campus dell'Hillsborough Community College, Campus di Ybor.

98-99	*Generations*, a mural on the campus of Hillsborough Community College, Ybor Campus	Courtesy of Hillsborough Community College, Ybor Campus, Department of Visual and Performing Arts, by artist Trinity Rivard	Generaciones (Generations), un mural en el campus de la Escuela Universitaria Comunitaria de Hillsbrough (HCC) Campus de Ybor	Generazioni, un murale nel campus dell'Hillsborough Community College, Campus di Ybor.
101	Two photographs depicting shophouses on 7th Avenue with shops on the first floor and living quarters on the second level in the style of those in New Orleans	Photos by PS	Dos fotografías mostrando tiendas en la 7a Avenida con tiendas en el primer piso y viviendas en el segundo nivel al estilo de las de Nueva Orleans	Due fotografie mostrano le botteghe in Via 7° coi negozi al primo piano e alloggio al secondo piano in stile New Orleans.
101	Ink sketch of casitas by Nancy Henderson	From a notecard image, used with permission	Bosquejo de tinta de Casitas por Nancy Henderson	Schizzo d'inchiostro delle casette da Nancy Henderson.
102	The Norman style tower of the "The Castle"	Photo by PS	La torre al estilo Normando de "El Castillo"	La torre di stile normanno del "Castello".
102	Medieval looking building now known as "The Castle" in its current life as a nightclub, but was originally the Labor Union Hall	Photo by PS	Edificio parecido medieval ahora conocido como "El Castillo" en su vida corriente como un club nocturno, pero originalmente el Salón de Sindicato	L'edificio d'aspetto medievale noto come "Il Castello". Adesso divenuta una discoteca.
103	The Italian Club's east façade reflects the architectural features, which make the building unique	Photos by PS	La fachada este del Club Italiano refleja las características arquitectónicas, que hacen el edificio único	La facciata est dell'Unione Italiana riflette le caratteristiche architettoniche che rendono l'edificio unico.
104	The Cuban Club, whose structure dominates the corner with classical Greek revival elements	Photo by PS	El Club Cubano, cuya estructura domina la esquina con elementos clásicos del reavivamiento griego	Il Club Cubano, la struttura domina l'angolo con elementi classici della rinascita greca.
105	The Spanish Club, Centro Español de Tampa on E. 7th Avenue at N. 16th Street incorporates a variety of European styles	El Centro Español de Tampa, Public Domain Image, National Park Service, Wikimedia Commons, Ebyabe, Creative Commons Share Alike 3.0 Unported, 2.5 Generic, 2.0 Generic and 1.0 Generic license. Https://comons.wikimedia.org/wiki/File: Tampa_Centro_Expanol_de_Tampa01.jpg.	El Club Español, Centro Español de Tampa en la Avenida 7 Este en la Calle 16 Norte incorpora una variedad de estilos europeos	Il Club Spagnolo, Centro Espanol di Tampa con una varietà di stili europei, Via 7° est e la strada 16 nord.

106	El Pasaje (The Cherokee Club) (1886), means "passageway" and refers to the columns that line the front of the building	Photo by PS	El Pasaje (El Club Cherokee) (1886) significa "pasillo" y se refiere a las columnas que alinean el frente del edificio	Il Pasaje (The Cherokee club), 1886, significa "passaggio" e si riferisce alle colonne che fiancheggiano la facciata dell'edificio.
106	El Centro Asturiano de Tampa (1914), formed in 1902 from an extension of Centro Asturiano de La Habana, to support the Spanish immigrants for Asturias, is still active today.	Photo by PS	El Centro Asturiano de Tampa (1914), formado en 1902 de una extensión del Centro Asturiano de La Habana, para apoyar a los inmigrantes españoles de Asturias, todavía sigue activo hoy.	El Centro Asturiano de Tampa (1914) formato come un'estensione del Centro Asturiano per sostenere gli immigranti spagnoli di Asturias, ancora e' un club attivo
107	The German-American Club (1909), on N. Nebraska Avenue at N. 11th Street, resembles simpler architectural lines of the French Directorate period and American Federalist period	Photo by PS	El Club Alemán-Americano (1909) en la Avenida Nebraska Norte en la Calle 11 Norte, se parece líneas arquitectónicas más simple que la época del Consejo Administrativo Francés y la época del Federalista Americano	Il Circolo Tedesco-Americano (1909), Via Nebraska nord e la strada 11, assomiglia alle linee architettoniche più semplici del periodo del Direttorato francese e del periodo federalista americano.
107	The Columbia Restaurant with its loggias, Spanish tiles and stuccoed walls is an elegant contribution to the architecture of Ybor City	Photo by PS	El Restaurante Columbia con sus azulejos logias, azulejos españoles y paredes estucadas es una contribución elegante a la arquitectura de la Ciudad de Ybor	Il ristorante Colombia con le logge, piastrelle spagnole e pareti stuccate, contributo elegante dell'architettura della Citta' di Ybor.
108	Freestanding archway to Ybor City heralds the entrance from Tampa proper into Ybor City	Courtesy of Cooper Johnson Smith, Peterson, Architects & Town Planners	El arco independiente a la Ciudad de Ybor anuncia la entrada desde Tampa apropiada a la Ciudad de Ybor	L'arco indipendente della Citta' di Ybor annuncia l'entrata a Tampa nella città di Ybor.
108	Old macaroni factory, which has been transformed into Casa Santo Stephano's Sicilian cuisine restaurant, with its Italian villa features and garden at the drive-in-pick-up entrance	Photo by PS	La vieja fábrica de macarrones, que se ha transformado en el Restaurante de Cocina Siciliana de Casa Santo Stephano, con sus características de villa italiana y jardín en la entrada de conducir-en-recoger	La vecchia fabbrica di maccheroni, che fu trasformata nel ristorante di cucina siciliana, Casa Santo Stefano, con le caratteristiche di una villa italiana ed un giardino con entrata del drive -in pick up (portala via).
109	Gasparilla pirate ship moves up the channel with cannons blazing to enforce its demands on a welcoming city.	Courtesy of Dave Decker Photography	El barco pirata Gasparilla se mueve por el canal con cañones flameantes para imponer sus demandas en una ciudad acogedora	La nave pirata Gasparilla che naviga nel canale, con i cannoni in fiamme, per far rispettare le sue richieste ed essere ben accolta dalla città.

109	Pirate crew on board	Courtesy of Dave Decker Photography	La tripulación pirata a bordo	La ciurma pirata a bordo.
110	Members of the Tampa Bay Flamenco Dance Company performing on Fiesta Day.	Courtesy of the Tampa Bay Flamenco Dance Company	Miembros de la Compañía de Baile Flamenco de la Bahía de Tampa realizando en el Día de la Fiesta	I membri della Tampa Bay Flamenco Dance Company ballano nella Fiesta Day.
111	Sant' Yago Knight Parade featuring some of the Krewes of Ybor and local marching bands	Courtesy of Keir Magoulas, Visit Tampa Bay	Desfile de Caballeros de Sant' Yago presentando algunos de los Krews de Ybor y bandas de música locales	La parata dei cavalieri di Sant'Yago con alcuni Krewes di Ybor e le bande musicali locali.
112	Tampa Pride Parade brings the whole community together with a variety of events for the public to enjoy	Courtesy of Keir Magoulas, Visit Tampa Bay	El Desfile de Tampa Pride trae toda la comunidad junta con una variedad de eventos para el público, para disfrutar	Tampa Pride Parade riunisce tutta la comunità con una varietà d' eventi per il pubblico.
113	Cuban Sandwich Festival attracts all those in honor of Ybor City's most favorite food	Courtesy of Cubansandwichfestival. com	El Festival del Sándwich Cubano atrae todos aquellos en honor a la comida más favorita de la Ciudad de Ybor	Il Festival del Panino Cubano attira molta gente in onore del cibo più preferito della citta' di Ybor.
113	Cuban sandwich from Hotel Haya	Photo by PS	Un sandwich cubano del Hotel Haya	Un panino cubano del Hotel Haya
114	Mid November marks the tree lighting in Centro Ybor ushering in the season in earnest for the city	Courtesy of Michael A. Murphy	A mediados de noviembre marca la iluminación del árbol en Centro Ybor marcando el comienzo de la temporada en serio para la comunidad	Nella metà di novembre, c'è l'illuminazione dell'albero nel Centro Ybor che inaugura la stagione invernale per la citta'.
115	Serving crew relaxes after dispensing cookies and hot chocolate to the masses at the Tree Lighting in Centro Ybor	Photo used with permission	Tripulación de servicio se relaja después de repartir galletas y chocolate caliente a las muchedumbres en la Iluminación del Árbol en Centro Ybor	Il gruppo si rilassa dopo aver servito i biscotti e la cioccolata calda agli spettatori per l'illuminazione dell'albero nel Centro Ybor.
115	One of the marching bands at the New Year's Eve Parade	Courtesy of PamElla Lee Photography. Used with permission.	Una de las bandas de música en el Desfile de La Víspera de Año Nuevo	Le bande musicali nel parato di Capodanno.
116	On the evening of the Lighting of the Tree, 2023, a double rainbow precedes the first public event in Ybor City following a tragic October	Photo by PS	En la noche de la Iluminación del Árbol, 2023, un doble arcoiris procede el primer evento público en la Ciudad de Ybor, siguiendo un octubre trágico	Il primo evento dopo una tragedia in ottobre in Ybor City, appare un doppio arcobalano durante l'illuminazione dell'albero.

117	Interactive display of Al Lopez Field in the Tampa Baseball Museum at the Al Lopez House	Courtesy of Arminda Mata, President and CEO, Ybor City Museum Society	Exhibición interactiva del Campo Al López en el Museo de Béisbol de Tampa en la Casa Al López	Esposizione interattiva dell'Al Lopez Field nel Museo di Baseball alla casa di Al Lopez
118	Students visiting the José Martí Park	Courtesy of Tampa Bay Tours, Ybor City Historic Walking Tours	Estudiantes visitando el Parque José Martí	Alcuni studenti che visitano il Parco José' Martí'.
119	View of the interior of GameTime's gaming room	Photo by PS. Used with permission	Vista del interior de la sala de juegos de GameTime	La vista interna della sala dei giochi di Game Time.
119	Gift Shop area for kids of all ages at the Visitor Information Center	Photo by PS	Área de tienda de regalos para niños de todas las edades en el Centro de Información para Visitantes	Il magazzino dei regali per i bambini di tutte le età al Centro Turistico.
120	Streetcar stop at Centro Ybor station	Photo by PS	Parada de tranvía en la estación Centro Ybor	La fermata del tram alla stazione Centro Ybor.
121	DRIP Ybor - an opportunity to create in many mediums	Courtesy of DRIP Ybor, Jonathan Scanlon	DRIP Ybor - una oportunidad para crear en muchos medios	DRIP Ybor - un'opportunita' per creare in vari modi.
122	Dysfunctional Grace Art Co. on 7th Avenue	Photo by PS	Compañía de Arte Dysfunctional Grace en la 7a Avenida	Disfunctional Grace Art Company, in via 7°.
123	Brick street pattern in front of the Hilton Garden Inn	Photo by PS	Patrón de calle de ladrillo frente de la Posada Hilton Garden	La strada di mattoni in fronte all'albergo, Hilton Gardens.
123	Street lamp at night at the Ybor City Museum State Park	Photo by PS	Farol callejero, de noche en el Museo del Parque Estatal de la Ciudad Ybor	Lampione di notte nel parco statale della citta' di Ybor.
124	Rooster, hen, and chicks in the Hilton Garden parking lot	Photos by PS	Gallo, gallina y pollitos en el estacionamiento de Hilton Garden	Gallo, gallina e pulcini nel parcheggio dell'albergo, Hilton Gardens.
124	Streetcar departing Centro Ybor Station going west	Photo by PS	Tranvía saliendo de la Estación Centro Ybor yendo al oeste	Il tram in partenza dalla stazione di Centro Ybor in direzione ovest.
125	Three casitas on 9th Avenue adjacent to the Ybor City Museum State Park	Photo by PS	Tres casitas en la 9a Avenida adyacente del Parque Estatal del Museo de la Ciudad de Ybor	Tre casette in via 9°, vicino al Ybor City Museum State Park.
127	Seal of Ybor City created by Anthony ("Tony") P. Pizzo	Attribution in text	Sello de la Ciudad Ybor creado por Anthony ("Tony") P. Pizzo	Il Sigillo di Ybor City creato da Anthony (Tony) Pizzo.
127	Progress Pride Flag of the LGBTQ+ community	Attribution in text	Bandera del Orgullo del Progreso de la comunidad LGBTQ+	La bandiera di Progress Pride della comunità LGBTQ+.

127	The five globe streetlamp can be said to represent the five major immigrant groups to Ybor City	Courtesy of Keir Magoulas, Visit Tampa Bay	Se puede decir que la farola de cinco globos representa los cinco grupos de inmigrantes principales de la Ciudad de Ybor.	Il lampione di cinque globi che rappresenta i cinque gruppi principali degli immigranti di Ybor City
128	Image from the interior of the Florida Aquarium	Courtesy of Visit Tampa Bay	Imagen desde el interior del Acuario de la Florida	L'interno dell'Acquario della Florida.
128	Image from a fish tank of the Florida Aquarium, Matthew Nankervis in the forefront	Courtesy of Lynn Nankervis	Imagen de una pecera del Acuario de la Florida, Matthew Nankervis al frente	Immagine di un acquario dell'Acquario della Florida, Matthew Nankervis al fronte.
129	Sparkman Wharf	Courtesy of Keir Magoulas, Visit Tampa Bay	Muelle Sparkman (Sparkman Wharf)	Pontile Sparkman.
129	Tampa Riverwalk	Courtesy of Visit Tampa Bay	Paseo del Río de Tampa	La passeggiata al fiume di Tampa.
130	Henry B. Plant Museum on the campus of the University of Tampa	Courtesy of Keir Magoulas, Visit Tampa Bay	Museo Henry B. Plant en el campus de la Universidad de Tampa	Il museo di Henry B. Plant nel campus dell'Università di Tampa.
130	Glazer Children's Museum	Courtesy of Visit Tampa Bay	Museo de Niños Glazer	Glazer Museo dei bambini.
131	Tampa Museum of Art	Courtesy of Visit Tampa Bay	Museo de Arte de Tampa	Il Museo d'Arte di Tampa.
131	The Straz Center	Courtesy of Visit Tampa Bay	El Centro Straz	Centro Straz.
132	Armature Works	Courtesy of Keir Magoulas, Visit Tampa Bay	Obras de Armadura (Armature Works)	Armature Works.
133	Map of Downtown Tampa	Map used under license with Maptive/Google	Mapa del Centro de Tampa	Mappa del centro di Tampa.
133	Archway lights over 7th Avenue installed in 2023 bearing a "Y" monogram in the center	Photo by PS	Luces del arco sobre la 7a Avenida instaladas en 2023 con un monograma de "Y" en el centro	L'arco di luci in via 7°, installata nel 2023 con un monogramma "Y" al centro.
136	*Fearless Champions* sculpture honoring First Responders and those they helped survive 911	Photo by PS	Escultura Fearless Champions honra a Los Primeros Respondedores y a los que ayudaron a sobrevivir el 911	La Scultura Fearless Champions in onore dei primi soccorritori che hanno aiutato la gente durante 11 settembre
154	Dawn breaks in the east through the 7th Avenue Archway entrance to the historic district	Courtesy of Cooper Johnson Smith Peterson, Architects & Town Planners	El amanecer sale por el este, a través de la entrada del Arco de la 7ª Avenida, al distrito histórico	L'alba attraversa il arco dell'entrata alla via 7 nel quartiere storico

Dawn breaks in the east through the 7th Avenue Archway heralding another day in the history of Ybor City. Courtesy of Cooper Johnson Smith Peterson, Architects & Town Planners.

Topical Index

www.ingramcontent.com/pod-product-compliance
Lightning Source LLC
Chambersburg PA
CBHW041426120626
46547CB00002B/114